9000913761

How To Pronounce

French Rose Names

Diana Bellucci

First Edition

LUMINOSA
PUBLISHING

Luminosa Publishing, Inc.
La Jolla, California

How To Pronounce

French Rose Names
By Diana Bellucci

Published by:
Luminosa Publishing, Inc.
7660 Fay Ave., H-273
La Jolla, CA 92037

Orders: www.howtopronounce.com

SAN 254-9247

ISBN Print ed. 1-932253-05-X

First Printing 2002
Printed in the United States of America

Library of Congress Control Number: 2002095752
Bellucci, Diana
How To Pronounce French Rose Names/ Diana Bellucci
1. Gardening, Rose Gardening

Contents

Preface: Note to the Reader

This is an exciting time to be collecting antique roses. Combining the knowledge of today's passionate historians and collectors with the power of the Internet, we now have antique rose information at our fingertips.

This reference guide How To Pronounce French Rose Names brings it all together, providing a simple, easy guide to instill confidence when saying French and German rose names.

The pronunciations in this guide may not be "perfect" French and German, nor do they follow the confusing International guides for language phonetics. But, after much deliberation, I concluded that collectors living in the English-speaking world simply want the most basic phonetics and format to get the pronunciations "mostly" right.

Why "mostly" right instead of "perfectly" right? Because it takes much study and practice to grasp the proper phonetics required to speak French and German correctly.

I just want to have fun in my garden when I say the name of a rose, and I expect you do too. So, I hope this guide's lighthearted approach will help you pronounce your French rose names more closely to correct than before and you have fun with it.

Happy collecting and happy pronouncing!

Diana Bellucci, La Jolla, California

Acknowledgments

How can one begin to acknowledge all those responsible for the vast varieties of roses that fill our gardens today? Surely the list would be extensive if one includes every collector, admirer, poet, artist, and dreamer who has quietly strolled through both formal and casual rose gardens.

And who are the passersby who just had to stop and smell what some consider the world's most beloved flower? The perpetuating and proliferating interest by so many has kept the genus Rosa near our souls through times of uncertainty, times of peace, and times of passion.

Certainly the famed Empress Josephine of France deserves applause for her contribution to the hybridization and propagation of roses. So do the numerous cultures previous to our own—the pioneers and grandparents who shared our enthusiasm for roses.

As for help with this guide specifically, I must acknowledge those who provided information, emotional support, and stories of their own. Special thanks to:

- Lee Sherman, my mentor and friend, who imports rare bud wood into the United States for her collection of nearly 600 roses and for our country's commerce.

- The hybridizers, grafters, and dealers who make great efforts to get us baby roses every spring, including that one rose we just must have.

- The historians for their endless hours of research, the landscape designers with their artistic ability to "paint" with the vast pallet of bloom colors, and the "Texas Rose Rustlers" who ask permission before sampling the long lost beauties, then share their finds with us all.

- The South Bay Heritage Rose Group, Friends of the Guadalupe River Park and Gardens, and the City of San José for their efforts in creating the San Jose Heritage Rose Garden. I often lost myself in serene contentment in this magnificent rose garden. I also gratefully acknowledge numerous picturesque gardens and collections, both public and private.

- The American Rose Society and its local branch societies that offer a gathering place to discuss all things "rosy."

I thank you all—those mentioned and those missed—as I anticipate spring, fill my senses in summer, taste the fruits of autumn, and thoughtfully dream each winter about my favorite bloom of all, THE ROSE.

Credits

All copyrights, pronunciation guide keys, trademarks, and trade dress belong to Luminosa Publishing, Inc.

Grateful acknowledgment is made to the following publishers for permission to use their extensive lists as a guide:

Botanica's Roses ISBN 0 09 183803 7 First published in 1998, by Random House Australia Pty Ltd.

Combined Rose List 2002, by Beverly R. Dobson and Peter Schneider

Roses of the San Jose Heritage Rose Garden Catalog, 2002 ed., by The South Bay Heritage Rose Group

Publisher .... Luminosa Publishing, Inc.
Author ....Diana Bellucci
Editor .... Barbara McNichol
Cover Concept ....Diana Bellucci
Cover Graphic Design...........................Key Advertising Concepts
Page Layout ....Key Advertising Concepts
Printer ....Central Plains Book Manufacturing
Author's Photograph....................................... Scott Coffin
Chromolithographs ....Various Artists Public Domain
Rosebud Silhouette ....Diana Bellucci
French Teachers
    Team Leader...............................Anne-Laure Le Révérend
German Teachers
    Team Leader..Verena Seisun

Warning-Disclaimer

This book was designed to provide simple and easy pronunciations of French and German rose names. It is sold with the understanding that the publisher and author are not engaged in rendering legal, accounting, or other professional services. If legal or other expert assistance is required, the services of a competent professional should be sought.

It is not the purpose of this guide to teach the French or German language, nor to teach international phonetic standards, but instead to entertain, amplify, complement, and supplement other rose or language texts.

Every effort has been made to make this guide as complete and accurate as possible, but as roses are identified and brought to the attention of the author, it is realized that this may not be a complete list. There may be mistakes, both typographical and in content. Therefore, this text should be used only as a general guide and not as the ultimate source of information or as a complete list of rose pronunciations or names.

The purpose of this guide is to inform and entertain. The author and Luminosa Publishing, Inc., shall have neither liability nor responsibility to any person or entity with respect to any loss or damage caused, or alleged to have been caused, directly or indirectly, by the information contained in this book.

If you do not wish to be bound by the above, you may return this book to the publisher for a full refund.

How to Use the French Pronunciation Guide

The French Language is a little tricky for us English-speaking folks. That's why this guide was created—to provide an easy way to come close to the correct French pronunciation on your first try. With some practice, you might realize that it's not so hard after all. You might even become inspired to learn the French language fluently.

So start by reading the pronunciation as if it were an English word, but try to remember the following points as you say the names:

- The French J is pronounced like the "z" in azure or the "s" in measure.

- When you see (n) or (h), you should barely say the n or h sound. Instead, say the letter before it through your nose and just "think" about the n or h sound. It's that nasal resonance that we English speakers have so much trouble with when speaking in French.

- The French R is made at the back of the throat and sounds like your morning gargle.

- The French U is tricky and may take some practice. It is like a cross between the "ew" sound in chew and the "oo" sound in mood.

Many rose names are made up of multiple languages and often named in honor of dignitaries from countries like France, Germany, Spain, and Italy. When a rose seems like it was named by the French, we have indicated how to pronounce the name as the French would.

Additionally, you will notice there are no stressed or accented syllables. High accentuation in French words completely disappeared after the VII century AD! The final syllables carry a moderate degree of stress that is not reported in any dictionary, as French is not considered an accentuated language. It is, however, accentuated by the sentence rather than by the word. The language's moderate accentuation rule is simple: The emphasis goes on the last syllable of a word (e.g., "fleur" becomes "fluHR") or the last word in a group of words (e.g., "fleur bleu" becomes "fluhr BLUH"). Please check your French dictionary and compare it with English, Spanish, or German dictionaries. You'll see there is no accentuation sign (') in the French phonetic but there are signs of accentuations in English, Spanish, or German.

We are always learning and we are committed to accuracy. Therefore, we welcome your ideas, corrections, and suggestions. Please drop a note in the suggestion box on our website at www.howtopronounce.com so we can expand our research and make appropriate changes.

How to Use the German Pronunciation Guide

If you thought the French language was tricky, then you will really have fun with the German pronunciations. German is pronounced more energetically and forcibly than English or French.

Again, we've tried to create an easy guide so you can get close to the correct German pronunciation on your first try.

Using the same logic as you did with French names, read the pronunciation as if it were an English word, but remember the following points:

- The German Umlaut, pronounced [oom-laowt], is indicated by a double dot over a letter, like ü. If you see a letter u without the Umlaut, then it's pronounced "oo" like the word food. However, if you see it with the Umlaut, it's pronounced further in the front of the mouth with rounded lips. This is indicated with a soft "e" sound, so it looks like (e)oo and the "e" is barely pronounced.

- Pronounce the hkh with a strong current of breath in the throat.

- Pronounce the h(k)h with a strong current of breath at the front of the mouth. Again, just "think" of the (k) sound.

- Note the accented syllables in CAPITAL letters. The German language needs this accentuation for proper pronunciation.

- For "long" vowels, we have doubled the vowel, recognizing that the long or short vowel pronunciation can change the meaning of the word. For example, the word "stadt" becomes "shtaaht" in the pronunciation so you know to lengthen the vowel sound.

Have fun learning how to pronounce the German rose names!

Rose Notes:

La Belgique horticole,   ROSE (Noisette) BOUQUET D'OR.   Jard. franç.
1879, pl. XV.   (DUCHER).   Rustique.

Bouquet d'Or
[boo-keh dohr]

ABC FRENCH

A Feuilles de Chanvre   [ah fuh-yuh duh sha(n)vr]
A Feuilles de Chyanvre   [ah fuh-yuh duh shee-ya(n)vr]
A Fleurs de Rose Trémière de la Chine
                  [ah fluhr duh hroz tray-myehr duh lah sheen]
A Longs Pédoncules   [ah lo(n) pay-do(n)-kewl]
Abailard   [ah-bay-lahr]
Abaillard   [ah-bahye-ahr]
Abbaye de Cluny ®   [ah-bayee duh klew-nee]
Abbé Bramerel   [ah-bay brah-mrehl]
Abbé Lemire ®   [ah-bay luh-meer]
Abel Carrierr   [ah-behl kah-hryehr]
Acidalie   [ah-see-dah-lee]
Adair Roche   [ah-dayr hro-sh]
Adélaïde d'Orléans   [ah-day-lah-eed dohr-lay-a(n)]
Adèle   [ah-dehl]
Adèle Heu   [ah-dehl uh]
Adèle Pradel   [ah-dehl prah-dehl]
Adèle Prévost   [ah-dehl pray-vo]
Adeline   [ah-duh-leen]
Admirable   [ahd-mee-hrahbl]
Adrienne de Cardoville   [ah-dryehn duh kahr-do-veel]
Agathe Fatima   [ah-gaht fah-tee-mah]
Agathe Précieuse   [ah-gaht pray-syuhz]
Age Tendre   [ah-zh ta(n)-dr]
Agéna   [ah-zhay-nah]
Aïcha   [ah-ee-shah]
Aimable Amie   [eh-mahbl ah-mee]

Aimable Rouge	[eh-mahbl roozh]
Aimée Vibert	[eh-may vee-behr]
Air France Meidilandina ®	
	[ehr fra(n)s meh-dee-la(n)-dee-nah]
Air France	[ehr fra(n)s]
Al Moise	[ahl mwahz]
Alain	[ah-lah(n)]
Alain Blanchard	[ah-lah(n) blah(n)-shahr]
Alain, Climbing	[ah-lah(n)]
Alba Meidiland ®	[ahl-bah meh-dee-la(n)]
Alba Meidilandécor ®	[ahl-bah may-dee-la(n) day-kohr]
Albéric Barbier	[ahl-bay-reek bahr-byay]
Albert la Blotais	[ahl-behr lah blo-tay]
Albert la Blotais, Climbing	[ahl-behr lah blo-tay]
Albert Payé	[ahl-behr pay-yay]
Albert Poyet	[ahl-behr pwah-yeh]
Albertine	[ahl-behr-teen]
Alexandre Girault	[ahl-ehk-sa(n)dr zhee-ro]
Alexandre Laquement	[ahl-ehk-sa(n)dr lahk-ma(n)]
Alexandre Tremouillet	[ah-lehk-sa(n)dr truh-moo-yeh]
Alfred Colomb	[ahl-frehd ko-lo(n)]
Alfred de Dalmas	[ahl-frehd duh dahl-mah]
Alliance ®	[ah-lee-ya(n)s]
Alliance Franco-Russe	[ah-lee-ya(n)s fra(n)-ko hrews]
Almandet	[ahl-ma(n)-deh]
Alouette	[ah-loo-eht]
Alpaide de Rotalier	[ahl-payd duh hro-tah-lyay]
Alphée	[ahl-fay]
Alphonse Daudet ®	[ahl-fo(n)s do-deh]
Alsace ®	[ahl-zahs]
Alsace-Lorraine	[ahl-zahs lo-rehn]
Altair ®	[ahl-tayhr]
Amadis	[ah-mah-dee]
Amazone [Ducher]	[ah-mah-zon]
Amboise Paré	[a(n)-bwahz pah-hray]
Amédée Philibert	[ah-may-day fee-lee-behr]
Amélia	[ah-may-lyah]
Amélie Gravereaux	[ah-may-lee grah-vro]
Améthyste	[ah-may-teest]
Ami des Jardins	[ah-mee day zhar-dah(n)]

Amitié	[ah-mee-tyay]
Amour Ardent	[ah-moor ahr-dah(n)]
Amourette	[ah-moo-reht]
Anaïs Ségalas	[ah-nah-ees say-gah-lah]
Anaïs Ségales	[ah-nah-ees say-gahl]
Andalousien ®	[ah(n)-dah-loo-zyah(n)]
André Eve ®	[a(n)-dray ayv]
André le Notre ®	[a(n)-dray luh notr]
André Leroy	[a(n)-dray luh-hrwah]
André Leroy d'Angers	[a(n)-dray luh-hrwah dah(n)-zhay]
Anémone	[ah-nay-mon]
Anémone Ancienne	[ah-nay-mon a(n)-syehn]
Anémone Rose	[ah-nay-mon hroz]
Anémonoïdes	[ah-nay-mo-noeed]
Angèle Pernet	[a(n)-zhehl pehr-neh]
Angélique ®	[a(n)-zhay-leek]
Angélique Quétier	[a(n)-zhay-leek kay-tyay]
Angélus	[a(n)-zhay-lews]
Anita Pereire ®	[ah-nee-tah puh-rehr]
Anne-Aymone Giscard d'Estaing®	
	[ah-nay-mon zhees-kahr dehs-tah(n)]
Anne de Bretagne ®	[ahn duh bruh-tah-neey]
Annelise ®	[ahn leez]
Anne-Laure ®	[ahn lohr]
Anne-Marie Côte	[ahn mah-hree kot]
Anne-Marie de Montravel	
	[ahn-mah-hree duh mo(n)-rah-vehl]
Annerose	[ahn hroz]
Annie Beaufais	[ah-nee bo-fay]
Annie Vibert	[ah-nee vee-behr]
Anthony Meilland ®	[a(n)-to-nee may(h)-(y)a(n)]
Antigone ®	[a(n)-tee-gon]
Antique	[a(n)-teek]
Antique Rose TM	[a(n)-teek hroz]
Antoine	[a(n)-twahn]
Antoine Ducher	[a(n)-twahn dew-shay]
Antoine Rivoire	[a(n)-twahn ree-vwahr]
Antonine d'Ormois	[a(n)-to-neen dohr-mwah]
Aparte	[ah-pahrt]
Apéritif	[ah-pay-hree-teef]

Apogée ®	[ah-po-zhay]
Apolline	[ah-po-leen]
Apricot Parfait ®	[pahr-fay]
Aquarelle	[ah-kwah-rehl]
Aquitaine ®	[ah-kee-tehn]
Arabesque ®	[ah-rah-behsk]
Arbelle ®	[ahr-behl]
Arc de Triomphe	[ahrk duh tree-yo(n)f]
Archiduc Charles	[ahr-shee-dewk shahrl]
Archiduc Joseph [Bernaix]	
	[ahr-shee-dewk zho-zehf] [behr-nay]
Archiduc Joseph [Nabonnand]	
	[ahr-shee-dewk zho-zehf] [nah-bo-na(n)]
Archiduchesse Elizabeth d'Autriche	
	[ahr-shee-dew-shehs ay-lee-zah-beht do-treesh]
Ardoisée de Lyon	[ahr-dwah-zay duh lee-yo(n)]
Ariana d'Algier	[ah-ree-ah-nah dahl-zhyay]
Arielle Dombasie ®	[ah-ryehl do(n)-bah-zee]
Aristide Briand	[ah-rees-teed brya(n)]
Aristide Brield	[ah-ree-steed bree-ehl]
Aristobule	[ah-ree-sto-bewl]
Arlequin	[ahr-luh-kah(n)]
Armada	[ahr-mah-dah]
Armide	[ahr-meed]
Armorique Nirpaysage	[ahr-mo-hreek neer-payee-zahzh]
Arnaud Delbard	[ahr-no dehl-bahr]
Arromanches	[ah-hro-ma(n)sh]
Arthur de Sansal	[ahr-tewr duh sa(n)-sahl]
Arthur Hillier	[ahr-tewr ee-lyay]
Arthur Oger	[ahr-tewr o-zhay]
Artiste®	[ahr-teest]
As de Coeur	[ahs duh kuhr]
Assemblage de Beauté	[ah-sa(n)-blahzh duh bo-tay]
Assemblage des Beautés	[ah-sa(n)-blahzh day bo-tay]
Assiniboine	[ah-see-nee-bwahn]
Astre	[ah-struh]
Astrée	[ahs-tray]
Atida	[ah-tee-dah]
Atoll	[ah-tol]
Audace	[o-dahs]

Auguste Gervais	[o-gewst zhehr-vay]
Auguste Gervaise	[o-gewst zhehr-vehz]
Auguste Renoir ®	[o-gewst ruh-nwahr]
Auguste Roussel	[o-gewst hroo-sehl]
Augustine Guinoisseau	[o-gews teen gee-nwah-so]
Aurore de Jacques-Marie ®	[o-hrohr duh zhak mah-hree]
Aurore Sand	[o-hrohr sa(n)d]
Aurore	[o-hrohr]
Avalanche	[ah-vah-la(n)sh]
Avalanche Rose	[ah-vah-la(n)sh hroz]
Aventure	[ah-va(n)-tewr]
Aveu	[ah-vuh]
Aviateur Blériot	[ah-vyah-tewr blay-hreeyo]
Avignon	[ah-vee-neeyo(n)]
Azure Sea	[ah-zewr]
Baby Albéric	[ahl-bay-reek]
Baby Carnaval	[kahr-nah-vahl]
Baby Faurax	[fo-hrahks] [1.]
Baby Garnette	[gahr-neht]
Baby Grand	[gra(n)]
Baby Masquerade ®	[mah-skuh-rahd]
Ballade	[bah-lahd]
Ballet	[bah-leh]
Barcarolle	[bahr-kah-hrol]
Bardou Job	[bahr-doo zhob]
Baron de Wassenaer	[bah-hro[n duh]
Baron Ernest Leroy	[bah-hro(n) ehr-nehst leh-rwah]
Baron Giraud de l'Ain	[bah-hro(n) zhee-ro duh lah(n)]
Baron Girod de l'Ain sport	
	[bah-hro(n) zhee-hro duh lah(n) spohr]
Baron Girod de l'Ain	[bah-hro(n) zhee-hro duh lah(n)]
Baron J B Gonella	[bah-hro(n) J.B.]
Baronne Adolphe de Rothschild	
	[bah-hron ah-dolf duh hrot-sheeld]
Baronne de Bonstetten	[bah-hron duh]

[1.] We understand that the final "X" in "Faurax" is pronounced because the last name comes from the dialect of Provence.

Baronne de Rothschild	[bah-hron duh hrot-sheeld]
Baronne Edmond de Rothschild ®	
	[bah-hron ayd-mo(n) duh hrot-sheeld]
Baronne G. Chandon	[bah-hro(n) G. sha(n)-do(n)]
Baronne Henriette de Snoy	[bah-hron a(n)-ryet duh snwah]
Baronne Prévost	[bah-ron pray-vo]
Baronne Rothschild	[bah-hron hrot-sheeld]
Baronne Surcouf ®	[bah-hron sewr-koof]
Baroness Rothschild	[bah-hro-nehs hrot-sheeld]
Baronesse ®	[bah-hro-nehs]
Baronesse Nathalie de Rothschild	
	[bah-hro-nehs nah-tah-lee duh hrot-sheeld]
Baroque	[bah-rok]
Bayadère	[bah-yah-dehr]
Beau Narcisse	[bo nahr-sees]
Beaujolais Tea	[bo-zho-lay]
Beaulieu	[bo-lyuh]
Beauté de Billard	[bo-tay duh beey-ahr]
Beauté de Versailles	[bo-tay duh vehr-sahye]
Beauté Française	[bo-tay fra(n)-sehz]
Beauté Inconstante	[bo-tay ah(n)-ko(n)s-ta(n)t]
Beauté Tendre	[bo-tay ta(n)dr]
Beauté Virginale	[bo-tay veer-zhee-nahl]
Beauté	[bo-tay]
Bébé Fleuri	[bay-bay fluh-hree]
Bébé Lune ®	[bay-bay lewn]
Béké	[bay-kay]
Bel Ange	[behl a(n)zh]
Belami	[behl-ah-mee]
Bellard	[beh-lahr]
Bellart	[beh-lahr]
Belle Alliance	[behl ah-lee-ya(n)s]
Belle Amour	[behl ah-moor]
Belle Ange	[behl a(n)zh]
Belle Anglaise ®	[behl a(n)-glehz]
Belle au Bois Dormant	[behl o bwah dohr-ma(n)]
Belle Aurore	[behl o-hrohr]
Belle Blonde	[behl blo(n)d]
Belle Champenoise ®	[behl sha(n)-pnwahz]

Belle Coquette	[behl ko-keht]
Belle Couronée	[behl koo-hro-nay]
Belle d'Orléans	[behl dohr-lay-a(n)]
Belle de Baltimore	[behl duh bahl-tee-mor]
Belle de Crécy	[behl duh kray-see]
Belle de Dom	[behl duh do(n)]
Belle de Londres ®	[behl duh lo(n)dr]
Belle de Nuit	[behl duh nwee]
Belle de Remalard	[behl duh ruh-mah-lahr]
Belle de Ségur	[behl duh say-gewr]
Belle de Yebles	[behl duh yaybl]
Belle des Jardins	[behl day zhahr-dah(n)]
Belle des Jardins [Guillot]	[behl day zhar-dah(n)] [gee-yo]
Belle des Jardins [Vibert]	[behl day zhar-dah(n)] [vee.behr]
Belle Dijonnaise	[behl dee-zho-nehz]
Belle Doria	[behl do-hryah]
Belle du Seigneur ®	[behl dew say-neey-uhr]
Belle Époque [Fryer]	[behl ay-pok] [free-yay]
Belle Époque [Lens]	[behl ay-pok] [la(n)s]
Belle Galathée	[behl gah-lah-tay]
Belle Hélène	[behl ay-lehn]
Belle Herminie	[behl ehr-mee-nee]
Belle Isis	[behl ee-zees]
Belle Ivryenne	[behl ee-vree-ehn]
Belle Lyonnaise	[behl lee-yo-nehz]
Belle Meillandina ®	[behl may(h)-(y)a[n-dee-nah]
Belle Nanon	[behl nah-no]n]]
Belle of Berlin	[behl]
Belle Poitevine	[behl pwah-tuh-veen]
Belle Portugaise	[behl pohr-tew-gehs]
Belle Rosine	[behl hro-zeen]
Belle Rouge	[behl hroozh]
Belle sans Flatterie	[behl sa(n) flah-tree]
Belle Story ®	[behl]
Belle Sultane	[behl sewl-tahn]
Belle Thérèse	[behl tay-rehz]
Belle Vichysoise	[behl vee-shee-swahz]
Belle Villageoise	[behl vee-lah-zhwahz]
Belle Virginie	[behl veer-zhee-nee]
Bellevue ®	[behl-vew]

Belvédère	[behl-vay-dehr]
Bengale à fleurs vertes	[bah(n)-gahl ah fluhr vehrt]
Bengale animée	[bah(n)-gahl ah-nee-may]
Bengale animée des Anglais	
	[bah(n)-gahl ah-nee-may day za(n)-glay]
Bengale Centfeuilles	[bah(n)-gahl sa(n)-fuh-yuh]
Bengale Cerise	[bah(n)-gahl suh-reez]
Bengale d'Automne	[bah(n)-gahl do-ton]
Bengale Ducher	[bah(n)-gahl dew-shay]
Bengale Ordinaire	[bah(n)-gahl ohr-dee-nehr]
Bengale Rouge	[bah(n)-gahl roozh]
Bérangère	[bay-ra(n)-gehr]
Bérénice ®	[bay-ray-nees]
Bermuda Catherine Mermet	
	[behr-mew-dah kah-treen mehr-meh]
Bermuda Papa Gontier	
	[behr-mew-dah pah-pah go(n)-tyay]
Bernadette	[behr-nah-deht]
Bernadette Chirac ®	[behr-nah-deht shee-rahk]
Bernaix	[behr-nay]
Bernensis	[behr-na(n)-see]
Bernina	[behr-nee-nah]
Berthe Lévêque	[behrt lay-vehk]
Bicolore Incomparable	[bee-ko-lohr ah(n)-ko(n)-pah-rahbl]
Bijou ®	[bee-zhoo]
Bijou d'Or ®	[bee-zhoo dohr]
Bijou de Royat-les-Bains	
	[bee-zhoo duh rwah-yah lay bah(n)]
Bijou des Amateurs	[bee-zhoo day ah-mah-tuhr]
Bijou des Prairies	[bee-zhoo day preh-ree]
Bingo Meidiland	[been-go meh-dee-la(n)]
Bingo Meillandécor ®	[been-go may(h)-(y)a(n) day-kohr]
Bizarre Triomphant	[bee-zahr tree-yo(n)-fa(n)]
Blanc de Vibert	[bla(n) duh vee-behr]
Blanc Double de Coubert	[bla(n) doobl duh koo-behr]
Blanc Lafayette	[bla(n) lah-fahyet]
Blanc Meillandécor ®	[bla(n) may(h)-(y)a(n)-day-kor]
Blanc Pur	[bla(n) pewr]
Blanc Queen Elizabeth	[bla(n)]
Blanche	[bla(n)sh]

Blanche Cascade ®	[bla(n)sh kahs-kahd]
Blanche Colombelle	[bla(n)sh ko-lo(n)-behl]
Blanche de Belgique	[bla(n)sh duh behl-zheek]
Blanche de Vibert	[bla(n)sh duh vee-behr]
Blanche Lafitte	[bla(n)sh la-feet]
Blanche Mallerin	[bla(n)sh mahl-rah(n)]
Blanche Moreau	[bla(n)sh mo-hro]
Blanche Neige	[bla(n)sh nehzh]
Blanche Pasca ®	[bla(n)sh pah-skah]
Blanche Superbe	[bla(n)sh sew-pehrb]
Blanche Unique	[bla(n)sh ew-neek]
Blanchefleur	[bla(n)sh-fluhr]
Blandine Choupette	[bla(n)-deen shoo-peht]
Bleu Magenta	[bluh mah-zhah(n)-tah]
Blue Bayou ®	[bah-yoo]
Blue Bijou	[bee-zhoo]
Blue Parfum ®	[pahr-fah(n)]
Blush Boursault	[boor-so]
Blush Maman Cochet	[mah-ma(n) ko-sheh]
Blush Noisette	[nwah-zet]
Bobo	[bo-bo]
Boccace	[bo-kahs]
Bon Silène	[bo(n) see-lehn]
Bon Silène Blanc	[bo(n) see-lehn bla(n)]
Bon Voyage	[bo(n) vwah-yahzh]
Bon-Bon	[bo(n) bo(n)]
Bonne Nouvelle	[bon noo-vehl]
Bonne Nuit	[bon nwee]
Bonsoir	[bo(n) swahr]
Borderer	[bohr-dhray]
Bordure Blanche ®	[bohr-dewr bla(n)sh]
Bordure Camaïeu ®	[bohr-dewr kah-mah-yuh]
Bordure d'Or ®	[bohr-dewr dohr]
Bordure Nacrée ®	[bohr-dewr nah-kray]
Bordure Rose ®	[bohr-dewr hroz]
Bordure Vermillion ®	[bohr-dewr vehr-meeyo(n)]
Bordure Vive ®	[bohr-dewr veev]
Bossuet	[bo-seweh]
Botaniste Abrial	[bo-tah-neest ah-breeahl]
Boudoir	[boo-dwahr]

Bougainville	[boo-gah(n)-veel]
Boule de Nanteuil	[bool duh na(n)-tuh-yuh]
Boule de Neige	[bool duh nehzh]
Bouquet d'Or	[boo-keh dohr]
Bouquet de la Mariée	[boo-keh duh lah mah-ryay]
Bouquet de Vénus	[boo-keh duh vay-new-s]
Bouquet Fait ®	[boo-keh fee-nahl]
Bouquet Parfait ®	[boo-keh pahr-fay]
Bouquet Tout Fait	[boo-keh too fay]
Bouquet Vanille ®	[boo-keh vah-neey]
Bouquetterie	[boo-keht-tree]
Bourbon Rose	[boohr-bo(n) hroz]
Bourgogne ®	[boohr-go-neey]
Bournonville	[boohr-no]n]-veel]
Bruxelles	[brew(k)-sehl]
Cachet TM	[kah-sheh]
Caen la Paix ®	[ka(n) lah pay]
Café	[kah-fay]
Café Olé	[kah-fay o-lay]
Caïd	[kah-eed]
Calypso	[kah-leep-so]
Camaïeux	[kah-mah-yuh]
Camaïeux Réversion	[kah-mah-yuh ray-vehr-seeyo(n)]
Camargue ®	[kah-mahrg]
Camélia Rose	[kah-may-lee-yah hroz]
Camelot	[kahm-lo]
Camille Pissarro ®	[kah-meey pee-sah ro]
Campanile ®	[ka(n)-pah-neel]
Can-Can	[ka(n)-ka(n)]
Candeur	[ka(n)-duhr]
Candeur Lyonnaise	[ka(n)-duhr lee-yo-nehz]
Candida	[ka(n)-dee-dah]
Cannes Festival ®	[kahn feh-stee-vahl]
Capitaine Basroger	[kah-pee-tehn bah-hro-zhay]
Capitaine Dyel de Gaville	
	[kah-pee-tehn dee-ehl duh gah-veel]
Capitaine Dyel, de Graville	
	[kah-pee-tehn dee-ehl duh gah-veel]
Capitaine John Ingram	[kah-pee-tehn]
Capitaine Williams	[kah-pee-tehn wee-lyahm]

Capitole ®	[kah-pee-tol]
Capri	[kah-pree]
Caprice [Meilland 1948]	[kah-prees] [may(h)-(y)a(n)]
Caprice [Meilland 1988]	[kah-prees] [may(h)-(y)a(n)]
Caprice de Meilland	[kah-prees duh may(h)-(y)a(n)]
Cardinal de Richelieu	[kahr-dee-nahl duh hreesh-lyuh]
Cardinal Hume ®	[kahr-dee-nahl ewm]
Carmeline ®	[kahr-muh-leen]
Carmen ®	[kahr-mehn]
Carmosine	[kahr-mo-zeen]
Carnaval	[kahr-nah-vahl]
Caroline	[kah-hro-leen]
Caroline Berry	[kah-hro-leen beh-ree]
Caroline de Berry	[kah-hro-leen duh beh-ree]
Caroline de Monaco ®	[kah-hro-leen duh beh-ree]
Caroline de Sansal	[kah-hro-leen duh sa(n)-sahl]
Caroline J.	[kah-hro-leen J]
Caroline Marniesse	[kah-hro-leen mahr-nee-yehs]
Caroline Rose	[kah-hro-leen hroz]
Caroubier	[kah-hroo-byay]
Carrousel	[kah-hroo-zehl]
Carte Blanche	[kahrt bla(n)sh]
Carte d'Or	[kahrt dohr]
Carte Noire ®	[kahrt nwahr]
Casimir Moulle	[kah-zee-meer mool]
Casque d'Or ®	[kahsk dohr]
Cassandre ®	[kah-sa(n)dr]
Castel	[kahs-tehl]
Catherine II	[kah-treen II]
Catherine Bonnard	[kah-stehl]
Catherine Deneuve ®	[kah-treen duh-nuhv]
Catherine Ghislaine	[kah-treen zhees-lehn]
Catherine Guillot	[kah-treen gee-yo]
Catherine Mermet	[kah-treen mehr-meh]
Cavalcade	[kah-vahl-kahd]
Cécile Brunner	[say-seel brew-nay]
Cécile Brunner White	[say-seel brew-nay]
Céleste	[say-lehst]
Céline Delbard ®	[say-leen dehl-bahr]
Céline Forestier	[say-leen foh-rehs-tyay]

Centenaire de Lourdes ®   [sa(n)-tuh-nehr duh loohrd]
Centenaire de Lourdes Rouge ®
                                 [sa(n)-tnehr duh loohrd hroozh]
Centfeuille   [sa(n)-fuh-yuh]
Centfeuille des Peintres   [sa(n)-fuh-yuh day pah(n)tr]
Centifolia à Fleurs Doubles Violettes
                       [sa(n)-tee-fo-lyah ah fluhr doobl veeyo-leht]
Cerise Bouquet   [suh-hreez boo-keh]
Cerisette la Jolie   [suh-hree-zeht lah zho-lee]
Césonie   [say-zo-nee]
Cévennes   [say-vehn]
Cézanne   [seh-zahn]
Chablis   [shah-blee]
Chaim Soutine   [soo-teen]
Chamois Dore ®   [shah-mwah dohr]
Champagne   [sha(n)-pah-neey]
Champagner ®   [sha(n)-pah-neey-ay]
Champlain   [sha(n)-plah(n)]
Champs-Élysées ®   [sha(n)-zay-lee-zay]
Champs-Élysées, Climbing   [sha(n)-zay-lee-zay]
Chanelle   [shah-nehl]
Chanson d'Été   [sha(n)-so(n) day-tay]
Chantal Mérieux ®   [sha(n)-tahl may-hryuh]
Chantebrise   [sha(n)t-breez]
Chantilly Lace   [sha(n)-teey-ee]
Châpeau de Napoléon   [shah-po duh nah-po-lay-o(n)]
Chardony ®   [shahr-do-nee]
Chardonnay   [shahr-do-nay]
Charlemagne   [shahr-luh-mah-neey]
Charles Bonnet   [shahrl bo-neh]
Charles de Gaulle ®   [shahrl duh gol]
Charles de Lapisse   [shahrl duh lah-pees]
Charles de Mills   [shahrl duh]
Charles Dingee   [shahrl]
Charles Lefébvre   [shahrl luh-fayvr]
Charles Mallerin   [shahrl mahl-rah(n)]
Charles Walker's Mignonette   [mee-neeyo-neht]
Charlotte [Austin]   [shahr-lot]
Charlotte [Duehrsen]   [shahr-lot]
Charme de Vienne   [shahrm duh vyehn]

Chartreuse	[shahr-truhz]
Chartreuse de Parme ®	[shahr-truhz duh pahrm]
Château d'Amboise ®	[shah-to da(n)-bwaz]
Château de Bagnois ®	[shah-to duh bah-neeywah]
Château de Beauregard ®	[shah-to duh bo-hruh-gahr]
Château de Chenonceaux	[shah-to duh shuh-no(n)-so]
Château de Clos Vougeot	[shah-to duh klo voo-zho]
Château de Clos Vougeot, Climbing	
	[shah-to duh klo voo-zho]
Château de Filain	[shah-to duh fee-lah(n)]
Château de la Juvenie	[shah-to duh lah zhew-vnee]
Château de Namur	[shah-to duh nah-mewr]
Château de Vaire	[shah-to duh vehr]
Château de Versailles ®	[shah-to duh vehr-sahye]
Château Frontenac	[shah-to fro(n)t-nahk]
Château la Croix	[shah-to lah krwah]
Château La Salle	[shah-to lah sahl]
Châteauroux	[sha-to-hroo]
Châtelaine	[shah-tlehn]
Châtillon Rambler	[shah-teeyo(n) hra(n)-blay]
Châtillon Rose	[shah-teeyo(n) hrozh]
Chénédolé	[shay-nay-do-lay]
Chère Michelle	[shehr mee-shehl]
Chevreuse ®	[shuh-vruhz]
Chic	[sheek]
Chimène ®	[shee-mehn]
Chivalry ®	[shee-vahl-ree]
Christian Dior	[krees-tya(n) dyohr]
Christian Dior, Climbing	[krees-tya(n) dyohr]
Christoph Colomb	[kree-stof ko-lo(n)]
Christophe Colomb, Gpt ®	[kree-stof ko-lo(n)]
Cicely Lascelles	[see-slee lah-sehl]
Ciel Bleu ®	[syehl bluh]
Cinéraire	[see-nay-hrehr]
Circé	[seer-say]
Citron-fraise ®	[see-tro(n) frehz]
Clair de Lune	[klehr duh lewn]
Clair Matin ®	[klehr mah-tah(n)]
Claire Jacquier	[klehr zhah-kyay]
Claire Rose ®	[klehr hroz]

Claire Laberge	[klehr lah-behrzh]
Claire Rayner	[klehr ray-nay]
Claude Monet ®	[klod mo-neh]
Clémentine Séringe	[klay-ma(n)-teen say-rah(n)zh]
Clos Fleuri Blanc	[klo fluh-hree bla(n)]
Clos Fleuri Champagne	[klo fluh-hree sha(n)-pahneey]
Clos Fleuri d'Or	[klo fluh-hree dohr]
Clos Fleuri ® Jaune	[klo fluh-hree zhon]
Clos Fleuri ® Rouge	[klo fluh-hree roozh]
Clos Vougeot ®	[klo voo-zho]
Clotilde Soupert	[klo-teeld soo-pehr]
Cocorico	[ko-ko-hree-ko]
Cocorico 1989	[ko-ko-hree-ko]
Coeur d'Alène	[kuhr dah-lehn]
Coeur d'Amour ®	[kuhr dah-moor]
Cognac	[ko-nyahk]
Colette ®	[ko-leht]
Colette Clémente	[ko-leht klay-ma(n)t]
Colibre ®	[ko-leebr]
Colibri	[ko-lee-bree]
Colibri 1979	[ko-lee-bree]
Cologne	[ko-loneey]
Comice de Tarn-et-Garonne	[ko-mees duh tahrn ay gah-hron]
Commandant Beaurepaire	[ko-ma(n)-da(n) bo-hruh-pehr]
Commandant Cousteau ®	[ko-ma(n)-da(n) koos-to]
Comte Boula de Nanteuil	
	[ko(n)t boo-lah duh na(n)-tuh-yuh]
Comte de Chambord	[ko(n)t duh sha(n)-bohr]
Comte de Falloux	[ko(n)t duh fah-loo]
Comte de Nanteuil [Quetier]	
	[ko(n)t duh na(n)-tuh-yuh] [kuh-tyay]
Comte de Nanteuil [Roeser]	[ko(n)t duh na(n)-tuh-yuh]
Comte de Sembui	[ko(n)t duh sa(n)-bwee]
Comte Foy	[ko(n)t fwah]
Comte Foy de Rouen	[ko(n)t fwah duh hroo-a(n)]
Comtes de Champagne	[ko(n)t duh sha(n)-pahneey]
Comtesse Branicka	[ko(n)-tehs brah-nee-kah]
Comtesse Brigitte Chandon-Moet ®	
	[ko(n)-tehs bree-zheet sha(n)-do(n) mweht]

Comtesse Brigitte de la Rochefoucauld ®
        [ko(n)-tehs bree-zheet duh lah hrosh-foo-ko]
Comtesse Cécile de Chabrillant
        [ko(n)-tehs say-seel duh shah-bree-ya(n)]

Comtesse de Barbantane	[ko(n)-tehs duh bahr-ba(n)-tahn]
Comtesse de Caserta	[ko(n)-tehs duh kah-sehr-tah]
Comtesse de Cassagne	[ko(n)-tehs duh kah-saneey]
Comtesse de Caÿla	[ko(n)-tehs duh]
Comtesse de Galard-Béarn	[ko(n)-tehs duh gah-lahr bay-ahrn]
Comtesse de Labarthe	[ko(n)-tehs duh lah-bahrt]
Comtesse de Lacépède	[ko(n)-tehs duh lah-say-pehd]
Comtesse de Leusse	[ko(n)-tehs duh luhs]
Comtesse de Murinais	[ko(n)-tehs duh mew-hree-nay]
Comtesse de Noghera	[ko(n)-tehs duh no-guh-hrah]
Comtesse de Oxford	[ko(n)-tehs duh]
Comtesse de Provence TM	[ko(n)-tehs duh pro-va(n)s]
Comtesse de Rocquigny	[ko(n)-tehs duh hro-kee-neey]
Comtesse de Ségur ®	[ko(n)-tehs duh say-gewr]
Comtesse de Woronzoff	[ko(n)-tehs duh vo-hro(n)-zof]
Comtesse des Bourbons	[ko(n)-tehs day boohr-bo(n)]
Comtesse Diana ®	[ko(n)-tehs dyah-nah]
Comtesse Doria	[ko(n)-tehs do-hryah]
Comtesse du Barry ®	[ko(n)-tehs dew bah-hree]
Comtesse du Caÿla	[ko(n)-tehs dew]

Comtesse Emmeline de Guigne
        [ko(n)-tehs ehm-leen duh gee-neey]
Comtesse Festectics Hamilton   [ko(n)-tehs]
Comtesse G. de Roquette-Buisson
        [ko(n)-tehs G. duh hro-keht bwee-so(n)]

Comtesse Jeanne de Flandre ®	[ko(n)-tehs zhan duh fla(n)dr]
Comtesse O'Gorman	[ko(n)-tehs]
Comtesse Ouwaroff	[ko(n)-tehs oo-vah-rof]
Comtesse Riza du Parc	[ko(n)-tehs hree-zah dew pahrk]
Comtesse Vandal	[ko(n)-tehs va(n)-dahl]
Comtesse Vandal, Climbing	[ko(n)-tehs va(n)-dahl]
Comtesse Vandale	[ko(n)-tehs va(n)-dahl]
Concertino ®	[ko(n)-sehr-teeno]
Concerto ®	[ko(n)-sehr-to]
Confetti	[ko(n)-feh-tee]
Constance	[ko(n)-sta(n)s]

Coquette des Alpes	[ko-keht day zahlp]
Coquette des Blanches	[ko-keht day bla(n)sh]
Coralie	[ko-hrah-lee]
Cordon Bleu	[kohr-do(n) bluh]
Cornélie	[kohr-nay-lee]
Coronet	[koh-hro-neh]
Corsair	[kohr-sehr]
Corso	[kohr-so]
Cortège ®	[kohr-tehzg]
Corvette TM	[kohr-veht]
Cosmopoliet	[kos-mo-po-lyeh]
Côte d'Azur	[kot dah-zewr]
Côte Jardins ®	[kot zhahr-dah(n)]
Cotillon TM	[ko-teeyo(n)]
Coucou®	[koo-koo]
Coup d'Hébé	[koo day-bay]
Coup de Coeur ®	[koo duh kuhr]
Coup de Foudre	[koo duh foodr]
Coupe de Parfum	[koop duh pahr-fah(n)]
Courier	[koo-hryay]
Couronne d'Or	[koo-hron dohr]
Courtoisie ®	[koohr-twah-zee]
Courvoisier	[koohr-vwah-zyay]
Cramoisi des Alpes	[krah-mwah-zee day zahlp]
Cramoisi éblouissant	[krah-mwah-zee ay-bloo-wee-sa(n)]
Cramoisi foncé velouté	
	[krah-mwah-zee fo(n)-say vuh-loo-tay]
Cramoisi Picoté	[krah-mwah-zee pee-ko-tay]
Cramoisi Supérieur	[krah-mwah-zee sew-pay-ryuhr]
Cramoisi Supérieur, Climbing	[krah-mwah-zee sew-pay-ryuhr]
Crème de la Crème	[krehm duh lah krehm]
Crêpe de Chine ®	[crehp duh sheen]
Crêpe Rose	[crehp hroz]
Crépuscule	[kray-pew-skewl]
Cricri	[kree-kree]
Crimson Boursault	[krah(n)-so(n) boohr-so]
Criterion	[kree-tuh-hreeyo(n)]
Criterion, Climbing	[kree-tuh-hreeyo(n)]
Croix Blanc	[krwah bla(n)]
Croix Blanche	[krwah bla(n)sh]

Croix d'Or	[krwah dohr]
Croix d'Or, Climbing	[krwah dohr]
Cuisse de Nymphe	[kwees duh nah(n)f]
Cuisse de Nymphe Émue	[kwees duh nah(n)f ay-mew]
Cybelle ®	[see-behl]
Cyclamen Meillandécor ®	

[see-klah-mehn] may(h)-(y)a(n)-day-kohr]

REVUE DE L'HORTICULTURE BELGE ET ÉTRANGÈRE

ROSE FÉLICITÉ PERPÉTUE

Félicité Perpétue
[fay-lee-see-tay pehr-pay-tew]

DEF FRENCH

D'Aguesseau	[dah-guh-so]
D'Arcet	[dahr-seh]
D'Artagnan ®	[dahr-tah-neeya(n)]
Dame Blanche	[dahm bla(n)sh]
Dame de Coeur	[dahm duh kuhr]
Dame de Coeur, Climbing	[dahm duh kuhr
Dame de l'Étoile ®	[dahm duh lay-twhl]
Dame Prudence	[dahm prew-da(n)s]
Dan Poncet ®	[da(n) po(n)-seh]
Daniel Lacombe	[da(n)-yehl lah-ko(n)b]
Danse des Sylphes	[da(n)s day seelf]
Danse du Feu	[da(n)s dew fuh]
Daphné	[dahf-nay]
Dauphine	[do-feen]
De Candolle	[duh ka(n)-dol]
De Esmée	[duh ay-may]
De la Grifferaie	[duh lah greef-hray]
De la Maître-École	[duh lah mehtr- ay-kol]
De Meaux	[duh mo]
De Montarville	[duh mo(n)-tahr-veel]
Début TM	[day-bew]
Débutante	[day-bew-ta(n)t]
Déclic	[day-kleek]
Décor Arlequin ®	[day-kohr ahr-luh-kah(n)]
Décor Rose	[day-kohr hroz]
Décor Terrasse	[day-kohr teh-hrahs]
Décoration de Geschwind	[day-ko-hrah-seeyo(n) duh]

Déesse	[day-ehs]
Delambre	[duh-la(n)br]
Dentelle de Bruges ®	[da(n)-tehl duh brewzh]
Dentelle de Bruxelles ®	[da(n)-tehl duh brew(k)-sehl]
Dentelle de Malines ®	[da(n)-tehl duh mah-leen]
Des Peintres	[day pah(n)tr]
Descemet	[deh-smeh]
Deschamps	[day-sha(n)]
Desgaches	[day-gahsh]
Désirée ®	[day-zee-hray]
Désirée Parmentier	[day-zee-hray pahr-ma(n)-tyay]
Desprez à Fleur Jaune	[day-pray ah fluhr zhon]
Deuil de Duc d'Orléans	[duh-yuh duh dewk dohr-lay-a(n)]
Deuil de Paul Fontaine	[duh-yuh duh pol fo(n)-tehn]
Deuil du Dr. Raynaud	[duh-yuh dew dok-tuhr hray-no]
Diamant ®	[dyah-ma(n)]
Diane	[dee-yahn]
Diane de Poltiers	[dee-yahn duh]
Diorama	[dee-o-hrah-mah]
Directeur Alphand	[dee-hrehk-tuhr ahl-fa(n)]
Dirigeant	[dee-ree-zha(n)]
Dis moi qui je suis	[dee mwah kee zhuh swee]
Disque d'Or ®	[deesk dohr]
Docteur Brière	[dok-tuhr bryehr]
Docteur Debat	[dok-tuhr duh-bah]
Dr. A.J. Verhage	[dok-tuhr A. J. vehr-ahzh]
Dr. Briar	[dok-tuhr bryahr]
Dr. Brière	[dok-tuhr bryehr]
Domaine de Courson ®	[do-mehn duh koohr-so(n)]
Dometille Beccard	[do-mteey beh-kahr]
Don de l'Amitié	[do(n) duh lah-mee-tyay]
Douce Symphonie ®	[doos sah(n)-fo-nee]
Douceur Normandie ®	[doo-suhr nohr-ma(n)-dee]
Doux Parfum	[doo pahr-fah(n)]
Du Maitre d'École	[dew mehtr day-kol]
Du Pré Tell	[dew pray]
Du Roi	[dew hrwah]
Dubonnet	[dew-bo-neh]
Duc d'Angoulême	[dewk da(n)-goo-lehm]
Duc d'Orléans	[dewk dohr-lay-a(n)]

Duc de Bordeaux	[dewk duh bohr-do]
Duc de Bragance	[dewk duh brah-ga(n)s]
Duc de Cambridge	[dewk duh]
Duc de Cazes	[dewk duh kahz]
Duc de Constantine	[dewk duh ko(n)s-ta(n)-teen]
Duc de Crillon	[dewk duh cree-yo(n)]
Duc de Fitzjames	[dewk duh]
Duc de Guiche	[dewk duh geesh]
Duc de Marlborough	[dewk duh]
Duc de Rohan	[dewk duh hro-a(n)]
Duc de Sussex	[dewk duh]
Duc de Valmy	[dewk duh vahl-mee]
Duc de Wellington	[dewk duh]
Duc Meillandina ®	[dewk may(h)-(y)a[n-dee-nah]
Ducher	[dew-shay]
Duchesse d'Abrantés	[dew-shehs dah-bra(n)-tays]
Duchesse d'Albe	[dew-shehs dahlb]
Duchesse d'Angoulême	[dew-shehs da(n)-goo-lehm]
Duchesse d'Auerstädt	[dew-shehs duh]
Duchesse d'Istrie	[dew-shehs dees-tree]
Duchesse d'Oldenbourg	[dew-shehs dol-da(n)-boor]
Duchesse d'Orléans	[dew-shehs dohr-lay-a(n)]
Duchesse de Berry	[dew-shehs duh beh-ree]
Duchesse de Brabant	[dew-shehs duh brah-ba(n)]
Duchesse de Bragance	[dew-shehs duh brah-ga(n)s]
Duchesse de Buccleugh	[dew-shehs duh]
Duchesse de Cambacérès	
	[dew-shehs duh ka(n)-bah-say-hrehs]
Duchesse de Cambridge	[dew-shehs duh]
Duchesse de Dino	[dew-shehs duh dee-no)]
Duchesse de Germantes	[dew-shehs duh gehr-ma(n)t]
Duchesse de Grammont	[dew-shehs duh grah-mo(n)]
Duchesse de Montebello	[dew-shehs duh mo(n)-tay-beh-lo]
Duchesse de Portland	[dew-shehs duh]
Duchesse de Reggio	[dew-shehs duh]
Duchesse de Rohan	[dew-shehs duh hro-ha(n)]
Duchesse de Vallombrosa	[dew-shehs duh vah-lo(n)-brozah]
Duchesse de Verneuil	[dew-shehs duh vehr-nuh-yuh]
Ducrat	[dew-krah]
Duet	[dew-eh]

Duette ®	[dew-eht]
Duo Unique	[dew-o ew-neek]
Dupuis Jamain	[dew-pwee zha-mah(n)]
Dupuy Jamain	[dew-pwee zha-mah(n)]
Dynamite ®	[dee-nah-meet]
Dynastie ®	[dee-nah-stee]
Éblouissant Pol de Turbat	
	[ay-bloo-wee-sa(n) pol duh tewr-bah]
Écho	[ay-ko]
Éclair	[ay-klayr]
Éclipse	[ay-kleeps]
École d'Écully ®	[ay-kol day-kew-lee]
Édith de Murat	[ay-deet duh mew-hrah]
Edouard Pynaert	[ay-dwahr pee-nahr)
Églantine	[ay-gla(n)-teen]
Églantyne Jebb	[ay-gla(n)-teen]
Églantyne ®	[ay-gla(n)-teen]
Élie Beauvillain	[ay-lee bo-vee-yah(n)]
Élisa Boëlle	[ay-lee-zah bo-ehl]
Élisabeth d'Angleterre	[ay-lee-zah-beht da(n)-gluh-tehr]
Élisabeth	[ay-lee-zah-beht]
Élise Boëlle	[ay-leez bo-ehl]
Élise Fleury	[ay-leez fluh-hree]
Elle ®	[ehl]
Ellinor LeGrice	[eh-lee-nohr luh-grees]
Émanuel	[ay-mah-new-ehl]
Émanuelle	[ay-mah-new-ehl]
Emera Blanc	[bla(n)]
Émeraude d'Or	[ay-mrod dohr]
Émile Charles	[ay-meel shahrl]
Émilie Verachter	[ay-mee-lee]
Émilien Guillot	[ay-mee-leeah(n) [gee-yo]]
Éminence ®	[ay-mee-na(n)s]
Emma de Meilland ®	[ay-mah duh may(h)-(y)a(n)]
Emmanuella de Mouchy	[ay-mah-new-ehlah duh moo-shee]
Emmanuelle	[ay-mah-new-ehl]
Empereur du Maroc	[a(n)-puh-ruhr dew mah-hrok]
Empress Joséphine	[zho-zay-feen]
Enchanteresse	[a(n)-sha(n)-trehs]
Enfant de France	[a(n)-fa(n) duh fra(n)s]

Ensa de Rennes ®	[duh Rehn]
Escapade ®	[ehs-kah-pahd]
Espérance	[ays-pay-hra(n)s]
Esprit ®	[ehs-pree]
Estelle	[ehs-tehl]
Estelle de Meilland ®	[ehs-tehl duh may(h)-(y)a(n)]
Étain	[ay-tah(n)]
Été Parfumé ®	[ay-tay pahr-few-may]
Étendard de Jupiter	[ay-ta(n) dahr duh zhew-pee-tehr]
Étendard	[ay-ta(n) dahr]
Étienne Levet	[ay-tyehn luh-veh]
Étoile de Feu	[ay-twahl duh fuh]
Étoile de France	[ay-twahl duh fra(n)s]
Étoile de Hollande	[ay-twahl duh o-la(n)d]
Étoile de Hollande, Climbing	[ay-twahl duh o-la(n)d]
Étoile de Lyon	[ay-twahl duh lee-yo(n)]
Étoile de Mai	[ay-twhl duh may]
Étude ®	[ay-tewd]
Eugène de Beauharnais	[uh-zhehn duh bo-ahr-neh]
Eugène Desgaches	[uh-zhehn day-gahsh]
Eugène Fürst	[uh-zhehn]
Eugène Verdier	[uh-zhehn vehr-dyay]
Eugénie de Guinoiseau	[uh-zhay-nee duh gee-nwah-zo]
Évangéline	[ay-va(n)-zhay-leen]
Évêque	[ay-vehk]
Exposition de Brie	[ehks-po-zee-seeyo(n) duh bree]
Fabergé	[fah-behr-zhay]
Fabvier	[fah vyay]
Fantasia [Dickson]	[fa(n)-tah-zyah]
Fantasia [Kordes]	[fa(n)-tah-zyah]
Fantin-Latour	[fa(n)-tah(n) lah-toor]
Farandole	[fah-hra(n)-dol]
Farouche ®	[fah-hroosh]
Fée Clochette ®	[fay clo-sheht]
Fée des Neiges ®	[fay day nehzh]
Féerie ®	[fay-ay-hree]
Félicie	[fay-lee-see]
Félicité Bohain	[fay-lee-see-tay bo-ah(n)]
Félicité Bohan	[fay-lee-see-tay bo-a(n)]
Félicite et Perpétue	[fay-lee-seet ay pehr-pay-tew]

Félicité et Perpétue	[fay-lee-see-tay ay pehr-pay-tew]
Félicité Parmentier	[fay-lee-see-tay pahr-ma(n)-tyay]
Félicité Perpétue	[fay-lee-see-tay pehr-pay-tew]
Femme	[fahm]
Fennet	[feh-neh]
Ferdinand de Lesseps	[fehr-dee-na(n) duh leh-sehps]
Ferdinand Pichard	[fehr-dee-na(n) pee-shar]
Ferdinard Chaffolte	[fehr-dee-na(n) shah-folt]
Feria TM	[fay-hryah]
Ferline ®	[fehr-leen]
Fernandel	[fehr-na(n)-dehl]
Festival	[fehs-tee-vahl]
Festival Fanfare	[fehs-tee-vahl fa(n)-fahr]
Fête des Mères	[feht day mehr]
Fête des Mères, Climbing	[feht day mehr]
Fête des Pères	[feht day pehr]
Fêtes Galantes ®	[feht gah-la(n)t]
Feu d'Artifice	[fuh dahr-tee-fees]
Feu Follet ®	[fuh fo-leh]
Feu Pernet-Ducher	[fuh pehr-neh dew-shay]
Fièvre d'Or	[fyeh-vr dohr]
Figurine TM	[fee-gew-reen]
Fil d'Ariane ®	[feel dah-hryahn]
Finale	[fee-nahl]
Flamêche	[flah-mehsh]
Flammêche	[flah-mehsh]
Flammentour	[flah-ma(n)-toohr]
Fleur Cowles	[fluhr]
Fleur d'Amour ®	[fluhr dah-moohr]
Fleur de Peltier	[fluhr duh pehl-tyay]
Fleurette ®	[fluh-hreht]
Flacon de Neige	[flah-ko(n) duh nayzh]
Flocon de Neige	[flo-ko(n) duh nayzh]
Flore	[flor]
Florence	[flo-ra(n)s]
Foliacée	[fo-lyah-say]
Folie d'Espagne	[fo-lee days-pahneey]
Folies-Bergère	[fo-lee behr-zhehr]
Folle Courtisane ®	[fol koohr-tee-zahn]
Fontaine	[fo(n)-tehn]

Fontaine des Loups	[fo(n)-tehn day loo]
Fontainebleu	[fo(n)-tehn bluh]
Fortuné Besson	[for-tew-nay beh-so(n)]
Fraîcheur	[fray-shuhr]
Français	[fra(n)-seh]
France de Berville	[fra(n)s duh behr-veel]
France Inter	[fra(n)s ah(n)-tehr]
France Libre ®	[fra(n)s leebr]
Francine Austin ®	[fra(n)-seen os-tah(n)]
Francis Dubreuil	[fra(n)-sees dew-bruh-yuh]
François Coppée	[fra(n)-swah ko-pay]
François Crousse	[fra(n)-swah kroos]
François Drion ®	[fra(n)-swah dreeyo(n)]
François Foucard	[fra(n)-swah foo-kahr]
François Gaujard	[fra(n)-swah go-zhar]
François Guillot	[fra(n)-swah gee-yo]
François Juranville	[fra(n)-swah zhew-ra(n)-veel]
François Krige	[fra(n)-swah kreezh]
François Levet	[fra(n)-swah luh-veh]
François Michelon	[fra(n)-swah mee-shlo(n)]
François Rabelais	[fra(n)-swah hrah-blay]
Frédéric Chopin	[fray-day-reek sho-pah(n)]
Frédéric II de Prusse	[fray-day-reek II duh prews]
Frédéric Mistral ®	[fray-day-reek mee-strahl]
Fruité	[frwee-tay]
Fugue ®	[fewg]
Fulgurante ®	[fewl-gew-ra(n)t]
Fusilier	[few-zee-lyay]

Gloire de Dijon
[glwahr duh dee-zho(n)]

GHI FRENCH

Gabrielle	[gah-bree-yehl]
Gabriel Noyelle	[gah-bree-yehl nwah-yehl]
Gabrielle Noyelle	[gah-bree-yehl nwah-yehl]
Gabrielle Privat	[gah-bree-yehl pree-vah]
Gallique Nouvelle	[gah-leek noo-vehl]
Garçon	[gahr-so(n)]
Garnet	[gahr-neh]
Garnette	[gahr-neht]
Garnette Carol	[gahr-neht kah-rol]
Garnette Pin	[gahr-neht pah(n)]
Garnette Red	[gahr-neht]
Gavotte	[gah-vot]
Gavroche ®	[gah-vrosh]
Gay Débutante	[day-bew-ta(n)t]
Géant des Batailles	[zhay-a(n) day bah-tahye]
Général Allard	[zhay-nay-hrahl ah-lahr]
Général Berthelot	[zhay-nay-rahl behr-tlo]
Général Cavaignac	[zhay-nay-hrahl ka-vay-neeyahk]
Général Donadieu	[zhay-nay-hrahl do-nah-dyuh]
Général Duc d'Aumale	[zhay-nay-hrahl dewk do-mahl]
Général Gallieni	[zhay-nay-hrahl gah-lyay-nee]
Général Jacqueminot	[zhay-nay-hrahl zhahk-mee-not]
Général Kléber	[zhay-nay-hrahl klay-bay]
Général Labutère	[zhay-nay-hrahl lah-bew-tehr]
Général Lamarque	[zhay-nay-hrahl lah-mahrk]
Général Schablikine	[zhay-nay-hrahl shah-blee-keen]
George Cuvier	[zhohr-zh kew-vyay]

Georges Cassagne   [zhohr-zh kah-sah-neey]
Georges de Cadoudal   [zhohr-zh duh kah-doo-dahl]
Georges Vibert   [zho-hrzh vee-behr]
Georgette ®   [zhor-zheht]
Gerbe d'Or   [zhehrb dohr]
Gerbe Rose   [zhehrb hroz]
Ghislaine de Féligonde   [zhee-slehn duh fay-lee-go(n)d]
Gilbert Bécaud   [zheel-behr bay-ko]
Ginette   [zhee-neht]
Giscard d'Estaing   [zhees-kahr dehs-tah(n)]
Giselle   [zhee-zehl]
Gîtes de France ®   [zheet duh fra(n)s]
Gitte   [zheet]
Givenchy   [zhee-va(n)-shee]
Glendore   [gla(n)-dohr]
Gloire d'Orient   [glwahr do-hreeya(n)]
Gloire d'un Enfant d'Hiram
                   [glwahr dah(n) a(n)-fa(n) dee-hra(n)]
Gloire de Bourg-la-Reine [glwahr duh boohr lah hrehn]
Gloire de Bruxelles   [glwahr duh brew(k)-sehl]
Gloire de Chédane-Guinoisseau
                   [glwahr duh shay-dahn gee-nwah-so]
Gloire de Deventer   [glwahr duh]
Gloire de Dijon   [glwahr duh dee-zho(n)]
Gloire de Ducher   [glwahr duh dew-shay]
Gloire de France   [glwahr duh fra(n)s]
Gloire de Guilan   [glwahr duh gee-la(n)]

Gloire de l'Exposition de Bruxelles
           [glwahr duh layks-po-zhee-seeyo(n) duh brew(k)-sehl]
Gloire de Paris   [glwahr duh pah-ree]
Gloire de Rome   [glwahr duh hrom]
Gloire des Anciens ®   [glwahr day za(n)-syah(n)]
Gloire des Hellènes   [glwahr day zeh-lehn]
Gloire des Jardins   [glwahr day zhahr-dah(n)]
Gloire des Mousseuses per ARS [glwahr day moos-uhz]
Gloire des Mousseux   [glwahr day moo-suh]
Gloire des Polyantha   [glwahr day po-lee-a(n)-tah]
Gloire des Rosomanes   [glwahr day hro-so-mahn]
Gloire du Midi   [glwahr dew mee-dee]

Gloire Lyonnaise	[glwahr leeyo-nehz]
Goubault	[goo-bo]
Gourdault	[goohr-do]
Gourmet Popcorn	[goor-meh]
Gournault	[goohr-no]
Grâce de Monaco ®	[grahs duh mo-nah-ko]
Grand Amore	[gra(n) ah-mohr]
Grand Bouquet	[gra(n) boo-keh]
Grand Château	[gra(n) shah-to]
Grand-Duc Henri	[gra(n) dewk a(n)-hree]
Grand Duc Héritier de Luxembourg	
	[gra(n) dewk eh-ree-tyay duh lewk sa(n)-boor]
Grand Finale	[gra(n) fee-nahl]
Grand Gala ®	[gra(n) gah-lah]
Grand Hôtel ®	[gra(n) to-tehl]
Grand Impression TM	[gra(n) ah(n)-preh-syo(n)]
Grand Nord ®	[gra(n) nohr]
Grand Prix ®	[gra(n) pree]
Grand Siècle ®	[gra(n) syehkl]
Grande Centfeuille de Hollande	
	[gra(n)d sa(n)-fuh-yuh duh o-la(n)d]
Grande Duchesse Charlotte de Luxembourg	
	[gra(n)d dew-shehs shahr-lot duh lewk-sa(n)-boor]
Grande Duchesse Charlotte	[gra(n)d dew-shehs shahr-lot]
Grande Esther	[gra(n)d ehs-tehr]
Grande Henriette	[gra(n)d a(n)-ryet]
Grande Renoncule	[gra(n)d hruh-no(n)-kewl]
Grandmère Jenny	[gra(n)-mehr zhuh-nee]
Granny Savoie	[sah-vwah]
Graves de Vayres	[grahv duh vehr]
Gravin d'Alcantara	[grah-vah(n) dahl-ka(n)-tah]
Gravin Michel d'Ursel ®	[grah-vah(n) mee-shehl dewr-sehl]
Grimpant Clair Matin	[grah(n)-pa(n) klayhr mah-tah(n)]
Grimpant Danse de Sylphes	[grah(n)-pa(n) duh seelf]
Grimpant Exploit	[grah(n)-pa(n) ehks-plwah]
Grimpant Pierre de Ronsard	
	[grah(n)-pa(n) pyehr duh ro(n)-sahr]
Gros Choux de Hollande	[ghro shoo duh o-la(n)d]
Gros Provins Panaché	[ghro pro-vah(n) pah-nah-shay]
Grouse 2000	[grooz]

Grouse	[grooz]
Guillaume Gillemot	[gee-yom zheel-mo]
Guinée	[gee-nay]
Guinevère	[gee-nuh-vehr]
Guirlande d'Amour ®	[geer-la(n)d dah-moohr]
Guirlande Fleurie	[geer-la(n)d fluh-hree]
Guitare ®	[gee-tahr]
Guitare, Climbing	[gee-tahr]
Guy de Maupassant ®	[gee duh mo-pah-sa(n)]
Guy Laroche	[gee lah-rosh]
Guy Savoy®	[gee sah-vwah]
Harmonie	[ahr-mo-nee]
Helen Naudé	[no-day]
Helen Traubel	[tro-behl]
Hélène de Gerlache ®	[ay-lehn duh gehr-lahsh]
Hélène Maréchal	[ay-lehn mah-hray-shal]
Henri Barruet	[a(n)-hree bah-rew-eh]
Henri Foucquier	[a(n)-hree foo-kyay]
Henri Fouquier	[a(n)-hree foo-kyay]
Henri IV	[a(n)-hree]
Henri Martin	[a(n)-hree mahr-tah(n)]
Henri Matisse	[a(n)-hree mah-tees]
Héroïne de Vaucluse	[ay-hro-een duh vo-klewz]
Heureux Anniversaire	[uh-hruh zah-nee-vehr-sehr]
Hippolyte	[ee-po-leet]
Hippolyte Jamain	[ee-po-leet zhah-mah(n)]
Hommage d'Anjou	[o-mahzh da(n)-zhoo]
Homère	[o-mehr]
Honoré de Balzac ®	[o-no-hray duh bahl-zahk]
Honorine de Brabant	[o-no-hreen duh brah-ba(n)]
Honorine Lady Lindsay	[o-no-hreen]
Horace Vernet	[o-rahs vehr-neh]
Hovyn de Tronchère	[o-vah(n) dun tro(n)-shehr]
Huguenot	[ewg-no]
Hugues Aufray ®	[ewg o-fray]
Ile de France ®	[eel duh fra(n)s]
Image d'Épinal	[ee-mahzh day-pee-nahl]
Impatient ®	[ah(n)-pah-sya(n)]
Impératrice Eugénie	[ah(n)-pay-hrah-trees uh-zhay-nee]
Impératrice Farah ®	[ah(n)-pay-hrah-trees fah-rah]

Impératrice Joséphine	[ah(n)-pay-rah-trees zho-say-feen]
Impératrice Rouge	[ah(n)-pay-hrah-trees hrooz]
Incomparable d'Auteuil	[ah(n)-ko(n)-pah-hrabl]
Infante Marie-Thérèse ®	[ah(n)-fa(n)t mah-hree tay-hrehz]
Innocence	[ee-no-sa(n)s]
Insolite	[ah(n)-so-leet]
Intervilles ®	[ah(n)-tehr-veel]
Intrigue ®	[ah(n)-treeg]
Invincible	[ah(n)-vah(n)-seebl]
Ipsilanté	[eep-see-la(n)-tay]
Irène	[ee-hrehn]
Irène Bonnet	[ee-hrehn bo-neh]
Irène de Danemark	[ee-hrehn duh dahn-mahrk]
Irène Watts	[ee-hrehn]
Isabelle de France	[ee-zah-behl duh fra(n)s]
Isabelle Nabonnand	[ee-zah-behl nah-bo-na(n)

Revue Horticole.

Rose La Vierzonnaise.

La Vierzonnaise
[lah vyehr-zo-nayz]

JKL French

Jacque Esterel	[zhahk ehs-tuh-hrehl]
Jacque Porcher	[zhahk pohr-shay]
Jacqueline	[zhahk-leen]
Jacqueline du Pré	[zhak-leen dew pray]
Jacqueline Humery ®	[zhahk-leen ew-mree]
Jacqueline Nebout ®	[zhak-leen nuh-boo]
Jacque Amyot	[zhak ah-myo]
Jacques Cartier	[zhak kahr-tyay]
Jacque Porcher	[zhak pohr-shay]
Jacques Prévert ®	[zhak pray-vehr]
James Bourgault	[boor-go]
James Pereire ®	[puh-rehr]
Jardin de Giverny	[zhahr-dah(n) duh zhee-vehr-nee]
Jardins de Bagatelle ®	[zhahr-dah(n) duh bah-gah-tehl]
Jardins de France ®	[zhahr-dah(n) duh fra(n)s]
Jardins de l'Essonne ®	[zhahr-dah(n) duh leh-son]
Jardins de Valloires	[zhahr-dah(n) duh vah-lwahr]
Jardins de Viels Maisons ®	
	[zhahr-dah(n) duh vyehl may-zo(n)]
Jardins de Villandry ®	[zhahr-dah(n) duh vee-la(n)-dree]
Jardins et Loisirs	[zhahr-dah(n) ay lwah-zeer]
Jaune Desprez	[zhon day-pray]
Jean Bach Sisley	[zha(n)
Jean Bodin	[zha(n) bo-dah(n)]
Jean de la Lune	[zha(n) duh lah lewn]
Jean Desprez	[zha(n) day-pray]
Jean du Tilleux	[zha(n) dew tee-yuh]

Jean Ducher	[zha(n) dew-shay]
Jean Galbraith	[zha(n)]
Jean Gaujard ®	[zha(n) go-zhahr]
Jean Giono	[zha(n) zheeyo-no]
Jean Girin	[zha(n) zhee-hrah(n)]
Jean Guichard	[zha(n) gee-shahr]
Jean Lelièvre	[zha(n) luh-lyehvr]
Jean Marc	[zha(n) mahrk]
Jean Marc Rose	[zha(n) mahrk hroz]
Jean Marmoz	[zha(n) mahr-mo]
Jean Mermoz	[zha(n) mehr-moz]
Jean Noté	[zha(n) no-tay]
Jean Notté	[zha(n) no-tay]
Jean Rameau	[zha(n) hrah-mo]
Jean Soupert	[zha(n) soo-pehr]
Jeanne d'Arc	[zhahn dahrk]
Jeanne de Montfort	[zhahn duh mo(n)-fohr]
Jeanne LaJoie	[zhahn lah-zhwah] [1.]
Jeanny Soupert	[zhah-nee soo-pehr]
Jeunesse Éternelle	[zhuh-nehs ay-tehr-nehl]
Jocelyn	[zho-slah(n)]
Joëlle Marouani ®	[zho-ehl mah-hrwah-nee]
Johasine Hanet	[ah-neh]
Joie de Vivre	[zhwah duh veevr]
Jolie Comtoise ®	[zho-lee ko(n)-twahz]
Jolie Demoiselle	[zho-lee duh-mwah-zehl]
Jolie Môme ®	[zho-lee mom]
Joseph Sauvageot ®	[zho-zehf so-vah-zho]
Joséphine	[zho-zay-feen]
Joséphine de Beauharnais	[zho-zay-feen duh bo-ahr-nay]
Jour de Fête	[zhoohr duh feht]
Jubilée TM	[zhew-bee-lay]
Jubilé du Prince de Monaco ®	

[zhew-bee-lay dew prah(n)s duh mo-nah-ko]

[1.] We understand this rose is named for a woman in Texas. This information could not be verified by press time, so we offer both the French pronounciation and this note.

Jubliant	[zhew-blya(n)]
Jules Margottin	[zhewl mahr-go-tah(n)]
Julie d'Étanges	[zhew-lee day-ta(n)zh]
Julie de Mersan	[zhew-lee duh mehr-sa(n)]
Julie de Mersent	[zhew-lee duh mehr-sa(n)]
Julie Delbard ®	[zhew-lee dehl-bahr]
Julien Renoard ®	[zhew-lyah(n) hruh-no-ahr]
Juliet	[zhew-lyet]
Juliette Gréco ®	[zhew-lyet gray-ko]
Jupon Rose	[zhew-po(n) hroz]
Justine Ramet	[zhews-teen hrah-meh]
Karine Sauvageot ®	[kah-hreen so-vah-zho(n)]
Kathe Duvigneau	[dew-vee-neeyo]
Kronenbourg	[kro-na(n)-boohr]
L'Abondance	[lah-bo(n)-da(n)s]
L'Admiration	[lahd-mee-hra-seeyo(n)]
L'Aimant	[lay-ma(n)
L'Amitié	[lah-mee-tyay]
L'Arlésienne	[lahr-lay- zyehn]
L'Enchanteresse	[la(n)-sha(n)-trehs]
L'Enchantresse	[la(n)-sha(n)-trehs]
L'Évêque	[lay-vehk]
L'Impératrice Farah	[lah(n)-pay-hrah-trehs fah-hrah]
L'Indéfrisible	[lah(n)-day-free-zeebl]
L'Ingénue	[lah(n)-zhay-new]
L'Obscurité	[lob-skew-hree-tay]
L'Oréal Trophy	[lo-hray-ahl]
L'Orléanaise	[lohr-lay-ah-nehz]
L'Ouche	[loosh]
La Belle Alsacienne	[lah behl ahl-zah-syehn]
La Belle Distinguée	[lah behl dees-tah(n)-gay]
La Belle Marseillaise	[lah behl mahr-say(h)-(y)ehz]
La Belle Sultane	[lah behl sewl-tahn]
La Biche	[lah beesh]
La Blancheur	[lah bla(n)-shuhr]
La Bonne Maison	[lah buhn may-zo(n)]
La Brillante	[lah bree-ya(n)t]
La Caille	[lah kahye]
La Canadienne	[lah kah-nah-dyehn]
La Diaphane	[lah dyah-fahn]

La Duchesse	[lah dew-shehs]
La Favorite	[lah fah-vo-hreet]
La Follette	[lah fol-eht]
La Fraîcheur	[lah fray-shur]
La France de 1889	[lah fra(n)s duh]
La France	[lah fra(n)s]
La France, Climbing	[lah fra(n)s]
La Grande Parade	[lah gra(n)d pah-hrahd]
La Guirlande	[lah geer-la(n)d]
La Jolie	[lah zho-lee]
La Louise	[lah loo-weez]
La Maculée	[lah mah-kew-lay]
La Marne	[lah mahrn]
La Marseillaise ®	[lah mahr-say(h)-(y)ehz]
La Minuette	[lah mee-new-eht]
La Négresse	[lah nay-grehs]
La Neige	[lah nehzh]
La Noblesse	[lah no-blehs]
La Nubienne	[lah new-byehn]
La Nymphe	[lah nah(n)f]
La Pandite Duchesse	[lah pa(n)-deet dew-shehs]
La Parisienne	[lah pah-hree-zyehn]
La Perle	[lah pehrl]
La Plus Belle des Ponctuées	[lah plew behl day po(n)k-tew-ay]
La Pucelle	[lah pew-sehl]
La Reine	[lah hrehn]
La Reine de Hamburg	[lah hrehn duh]
La Reine Victoria	[lah hrehn veek-to-hryah]
La Revenante	[lah hruh-vuh-na(n)t]
La Roche aux Fées ®	[lah hrosh o fay]
La Rose	[lah hroz]
La Rose Bordeaux ®	[lah hroz bohr-do]
La Rose de York	[lah hroz duh]
La Rosée	[lah hro-say]
La Roxelane	[lah hrok-sehlahn]
La Royale	[lah hrwah-yahl]
La Rubanée	[lah hrew-bah-nay]
La Séduisante	[lah say-dwee-za(n)t]
La Sylphide	[lah seel-feed]
La Syrène	[lah see-hrehn]

La Tamponaise	[lah ta(n)-po-nehz]
La Tendresse	[lah ta(n)-drehs]
La Tosca	[lah tos-kah]
La Tour d'Argent	[lah toor dahr-zha(n)]
La Triomphe	[lah tree-yo(n)f]
La Venissiane ®	[lah vuh-nee syahn]
La Vierzonnaise	[lah vyehr-zo-nayz]
La Ville de Bruxelles	[lah veel duh brew(k)-sehl]
La Virginale	[lah veer-zhee-nahl]
Lac Blanc	[lahk bla(n)]
Lac Majeau	[lahk ma-zho]
Lac Rose	[lahk hroz]
Lafayette	[lah-fahyet]
Lamarque	[lah-mahrk]
Lambada	[la(n)-bah-dah]
Laminuette ®	[lah-mee-neweht]
Lamotte Sanguin	[lah-mot sa(n)-gah(n)]
Lampion	[la(n)-peeyo(n)]
Lancôme ®	[la(n)-kom]
Laque de Chine ®	[lahk duh sheen]
Latte	[laht]
Lauré Davoust	[lo-hray dah-voost]
Laurence Olivier	[lo-hra(n)s o-lee-vyay]
Laurette Messimy	[lo-hreht meh-see-mee]
Laurette	[lo-hreht]
Lavande	[lah-va(n)d]
Lavonde	[lah-vo(n)d]
Le Bienheureux de la Salle	
	[luh beeyah(n)-uh-ruh duh lah sahl]
Le Cid	[luh seed]
Le Grand Capitaine	[luh gra(n) kah-pee-tehn]
Le Grand Huit	[luh gra(n) weet]
Le Havre	[luh ahvhr]
Le Jacobin	[luh zhah-ko-bah(n)]
Le Météore	[luh may-tay-ohr]
Le Pactole	[luh pahk-tol]
Le Petit Orange ®	[luh ptee o-hra(n)zh]
Le Poilu	[luh pwah-lew]
Le Rêve	[luh hrehv]
Le Rire Niais	[luh hreer nee-yay]

Le Roitelet	[luh hrwah-tleh]
Le Rouge et Le Noir	[luh hroozh ay luh nwahr]
Le Soleil	[luh so-layh]
Le Triomphe	[luh tree-yo(n)f]
Le Vésuve	[luh vay-sewv]
Lecocq-Dumesnil	[luh-kok dew-meh-neel]
Léda	[lay-dah]
Légion d'Honneur ®	[lay-zhyo(n) do-nuhr]
Léon Lecomte	[lay-o(n) luh-ko(n)t]
Léonard de Vinci ®	[lay-o-nahr duh vah(n)-see]
Léonidas TM	[lay-o-nee-dahs]
Léonie Lambert	[lay-o-nee la(n)-behr]
Léonie Lamesch	[lay-o-nee lah-mehsh]
Léonie's Apolline	[lay-o-nee ah-po-leen]
Léonor de March	[lay-o-nohr duh mahrsh]
Léontine Gervais	[lay-o(n)-teen zhehr-vay]
Léopoldine d'Orléans	[lay-o-pol-deen dohr-lay-a(n)]
Leparfum	[luh pahr-fah(n)]
Les Amoureux de Peynet ®	[lay zah-moor-uh duh pay-neh]
Les Sables d'Olonne ®	[lay sahbl do-loneey]
Les Saisons d'Italie	[lay say-zo(n) dee-tah-lee]
Les Sjulin	[lay szhew-lah(n)]
Les Sulin	[lay sew-lah(n)]
Lesbos	[lay-bo]
Letellier	[luh-tehlyay]
Liaison	[lee-yay-zo(n)
Lieve Louise ®	[lee-uhv loo-weez]
Lili Marléne	[lee-lee mahr-layn]
Lilli Marleen ®	[lee-lee]
Lily de Gerlache	[lee-lee duh gehr-lahsh]
Lisa Marée	[lee-sa mah-hray]
Lisa Marie	[lee-zah mah-hree]
Liselle	[lee-zehl]
Lisette de Béranger	[lee-zeht duh bay-hra(n)-gay]
Louis Bernard	[loo-wee behr-nahr]
Louis Bourgoin	[loo-wee boohr-gwah(n)]
Louis Bugnet	[loo-wee bew-neeyeh]
Louis de Funès ®	[loo-wee duh few-nehs]
Louis Gimard	[loo-wee zhee-mahr]
Louis Jolliet	[loo-wee zho-lyeh]

Louis Mon Ami	[loo-wee mo(n) nah-mee]
Louis Pajotin	[loo-wee pah-zho-tah(n)]
Louis Pajotin, Climbing	[loo-wee pah-zho-tah(n)]
Louis Phillipe	[loo-wee fee-leep]
Louis Phillipe d'Angers	[loo-wee fee-leep da(n)-zhay]
Louis XIV	[loo-wee kah-tohrz]
Louise Cretté	[loo-weez kreh-tay]
Louise d'Arzens	[loo-weez dahr-za(n)]
Louise Gardner	[loo-weez gahr-nay]
Louise Odier	[loo-weez o-dyay]
Louise Pommery ®	[loo-weez po-mrhee]
Louise Verger	[loo-weez vehr-zhay]
Lucie Crampton	[lew-see kra(n)-to(n)]
Lucie Duplessis	[lew-see dew-pleh-see]
Lulu	[lew-lew]
Loulou de Cacharel ®	[loo-loo duh kah-shah-rehl]
Lumen ®	[lew-mehn]
Lumière	[lew-myehr]
Lustre d'Église	[lewstr day-gleez]
Lutin ®	[lew-tah(n)]
Lyon Rose	[lee-yo(n) hroz]

ROSE (HYBRIDE REMONTANTE) Monsieur JOURNEAUX (MAREST & FILS.)
Semis France. (Plein-air)
A. Verschaffelt publ.

Monsieur Journeaux

[muh-syuh zhoohr-no]

MNO FRENCH

Ma Fille	[mah feey]
Ma Mie	[mah mee]
Ma Ponctuée	[mah po(n)k-tew-ay]
Ma Tulipe	[mah tew-leep]
Madeleine Rivoire ®	[mah-dlehn ree-vwahr]
Madelon	[mah-d[uh]-lo(n)]
Mademoiselle TM	[mah-dmwah-zehl]
Madette	[mah-deht]
Magali	[mah-gah-lee]
Magic de Feu	[duh fuh]
Magic Meidiland	[meh-dee-la(n)]
Magic Meillandécor	[may(h)-(y)a(n)-day-kohr]
Magicienne 78 ®	[mah-zhee-syehn]
Majestueuse	[mah-zhehs-tew-uhz]
Majeure	[mah-zhuhr]
Majorette ®	[mah-zho-hrayt]
Malin Juane Delbard ®	[mah-lah(n) dehl-bahr]
Malin Rose Delbard ®	[mah-lah(n) hroz dehl-bahr]
Malin Rouge Delbard ®	[mah-lah(n) hroozh dehl-bahr]
Maman Cochet	[mah-ma(n) ko-sheh]
Maman Cochet, Climbing	[mah-ma(n) ko-sheh]
Maman Lyly	[mah-ma(n) lee-lee]
Maman Turbat	[mah-ma(n) tewr-bah]
Mamy Laperriere ®	[mah-mee lah-pehryehr]
Mandarine Symphonie ®	[ma(n)-dah-hreen sah(n)-fo-nee]
Manette	[mah-neht]
Manou Meilland ®	[mah-noo may(h)-(y)a(n)]

Manteau d'Évêque	[ma(n)-to day-vehk]
Manteau Pourpre	[ma(n)-to poohrpr]
Marbrée	[mahr-bray]
Marcel Bourgouin	[mahr-sehl boohr-gwah(n)]
Marcel Pagnol ®	[mahr-sehl pah-neeyol]
Marcel Pagnolin Europe	
	[mahr-sehl pah-neeyo-lah(n) uh-hrop]
Marcel Proust	[mahr-sehl proost]
Marcelle Gret	[mahr-sehl greh]
Marcelle Marchand ®	[mahr-sehl mahr-sha(n)]
Marcellin Champagnat	
	[mahr-suh-lah(n) sha(n)-paneeyah]
Mardi Gras	[mahr-dee grah]
Mardi Gras, Climbing	[mahr-dee grah]
Maréchal Davoust	[mah-hray-shahl dah-voost]
Maréchal Davout	[mah-hray-shahl dah-voot]
Maréchal du Palais	[mah-hray-shahl dew pah-lay]
Maréchal Foch	[mah-hray-shahl fosh]
Maréchal le Clerc	[mah-hray-shahl luh klehr]
Maréchal Le Clerc	[mah-hray-shahl luh klehr]
Maréchal Leclerc	[mah-hray-shahl luh-klehr]
Maréchal Niel	[mah-hray-shahl nyehl]
Marguerite Anne	[mahr-guh-hreet ahn]
Marguerite Brassac	[mahr-guh-hreet brah-sahk]
Marguerite Jamain	[mahr-guh-hreet zhah-mah(n)]
Marguerite de Roman	[mahr-guh-hreet duh hro-ma(n)]
Marguerite Desrayaux	[mahr-guh-hreet day-hray-yo]
Marguerite Guillard	[mahr-guh-hreet gee-yahr]
Marguerite Guillot	[mahr-guh-hreet gee-yo]
Marguerite Hilling	[mahr-guh-hreet]
Mariandel ®	[mah-hree-ya(n)-dehl]
Maribel	[mah-hree-behl]
Marie Adélaïde	[mah-hree ah-day-lah-eed]
Marie Antoinette	[mah-hree a(n)-twah-neht]
Marie Bugnet	[mah-hree bew-neeyeh]
Marie-Claire	[mah-hree klehr]
Marie Curie ®	[mah-hree kew-hree]
Marie d'Orléans	[mah-hree dohr-lay-a(n)]
Marie Daly	[mah-hree dah-lee]
Marie de Blois	[mah-hree duh blwah]

Marie de Bourgogne	[mah-hree duh boohr-goneey]
Marie de Saint Jean.	[mah-hree duh sah(n) zha(n)]
Marie de St Jean	[mah-hree duh sah(n) zha(n)]
Marie Dermar	[mah-hree dehr-mahr]
Marie Gauschault	[mah-hree go-sho]
Marie Gouchault	[mah-hree goo-sho]
Marie Guillot	[mah-hree gee-yo]
Marie Henriette Grafin Chotek	
	[mah-hree a(n)-hryet grah-fah(n) sho-tehk]
Marie Laforêt ®	[mah-hree lah-fohreh]
Marie Lambert	[mah-hree la(n)-behr]
Marie Legonde	[mah-hree luh-go(n)d]
Marie Leonida	[mah-hree lee-onee-dah]
Marie Louise	[mah-hree loo-weez]
Marie-Louise Velge	[mah-hree loo-weez vehlzh]
Marie-Luise Marjan ®	[mahr-zhan]
Marie Pavié	[mah-hree pah-vyay]
Marie Pavier	[mah-hree pah-vyay]
Marie Robert	[mah-hree hro-behr]
Marie Segond	[mah-hree suh-go(n)]
Marie van Houtte	[mah-hree]
Marie-Antoinette	[mah-hree a(n)-twah-neht]
Marie-Claire	[mah-hree klehr]
Marie-Claire, Climbing	[mah-hree klehr]
Marie-Jeanne	[mah-hree zhahn]
Marie-Victorin	[mah-hree veek-toh-rah(n)]
Marinette	[mah-hree-neht]
Marionette ®	[mah-hreeyo-neht]
Marlène Jobert ®	[mahr-lehn zho-behr]
Marmalade	[mahr-mah-lahd]
Marquis d'Ailsa	[mahr-kee dayl-sah]
Marquis de Balbiano	[mahr-kee duh bahl-byah-no]
Marquisette ®	[mahr-kee-zeht]
Martin des Senteurs ®	[mahr-tah(n) day sa(n)-tuhr]
Martine Guillot ®	[mahr-teen gee-yo]
Mascara TM	[mahs-kah-hrah]
Mascotte	[mahs-kot]
Masquerade	[mahs-kuh-rahd]
Masquerade, Climbing.	[mahs-kuh-rahd]
Maupertuis	[mo-pehr-twee]

Maurice Bernardin	[mo-hrees behr-nahr-dah(n)]
Maurice Lepelletier	[mo-hrees luh-pehl-tyay]
Mauricette	[mo-hree-seht]
Mauve Melodée	[mov muh-lo-day]
Mécène	[may-sehn]
Médallion ®	[may-dah-yo(n)]
Méduse ®	[may-dewz]
Meg Merrilles	[meh-hreey]
Meilland Décor Arlequin	
	[may(h)-(y)a(n) day-kohr ahr-luh-kah(n)]
Meilland Décor Rose	[may(h)-(y)a(n) day-kohr hroz]
Meilland Rosiga	[may(h)-(y)a(n)]
Mélanie Lemaire	[may-lah-nee luh-mehr]
Mélodie Parfumée	[may-lo-dee pahr-few-may]
Mémoire ®	[may-mwahr]
Ménage	[may-nahzh]
MénageMerci	[may-nahzh-mehr-see]
Mercédès ®	[mehr-say-dehs]
Mercedes Gallart	[mehr-seh-dehs gah-lahr]
Merci	[mehr-see]
Merle Blanc	[mehrl bla(n)]
Merlin	[mehr-lah(n)]
Mers du Sud	[mehr dew sewd]
Merveille de la Brie	[mehr-vay(h) duh lah bree]
Merveille de Lyon	[mehr-vay(h) duh lee-yo(n)]
Merveille des Rouges	[mehr-vay(h) day hroozh]
Message	[meh sahzh]
Messire Delbard ®	[meh-seer dehl-bahr]
Métropole	[may-tro-pol]
Michel Bonnet	[mee-shehl bo-neh]
Michel Bras ®	[mee-shehl brah]
Michel Cholet TM	[mee-shehl sho-leh]
Michel Hidalgo ®	[mee-shehl ee-dahl-go]
Michel Joye ®	[mee-shehl zhwah]
Michel Lis le Jardinier ®	[mee-shehl lee luh zhar-dee-nyay]
Michèle Meilland	[mee-shehl may(h)-(y)a(n)]
Michèle Meilland, Climbing	[mee-shehl may(h)-(y)a(n)]
Michèle Torr ®	[mee-shehl tohr]
Mignon	[mee-neeyo(n)]
Mignonette	[mee-neeyo-neht]

Mille et Une Nuits   [meel ay uhn nwee]
Millefleurs   [meel-fluhr]
Minouchette   [mee-noo-shet]
Mireille   [mee-hray(h)]
Mireille Mathieu   [mee-hray(h) mah-tyuh]
Mlle Andrée Worth   [mah-dmwah-zehl a(n)-dray]
Mlle Annie Wood   [mah-dmwah-zehl ah-nee]
Mlle Augustine Guinoisseau
     [mah-dmwah-zehl o-gews-teen gee-nwah-so]
Mlle Berger   [mah-dmwah-zehl bayhr-gay]
Mlle Berthe Lévêque   [mah-dmwah-zehl behrt lay-vehk]
Mlle Blanche Lafitte   [mah-dmwah-zehl bla(n)sh lah-feet]
Mlle Cécile Brünner   [mah-dmwah-zehl say-seel]
Mlle Claire Jacquier
     [mah-dmwah-zehl klehr zhah-kyay]
Mlle Claire Truffaut   [mah-dmwah-zehl klehr trew-fo]
Mlle de Dinant   [mah-dmwah-zehl duh dee-na(n)]
Mlle de Sombreuil
     [mah-dmwah-zehl duh so(n)-bruh-yuh]
Mlle Favart   [mah-dmwah-zehl fah-vahr]
Mlle Franziska Kruger   [mah-dmwah-zehl]
Mlle Geneviève Godard
     [mah-dmwah-zehl zhuhn-vyehv go-dahr]]
Mlle Honorine Duboc
     [mah-dmwah-zehl o-no-hreen dew-bok]
Mlle Jacqueline   [mah-dmwah-zehl zhak-leen]
Mlle Jeanne Philippe   [mah-dmwah-zehl zhahn fee-leep]
Mlle Joséphine Guyet
     [mah-dmwah-zehl zho-zay-feen geeyeh]
Mlle la Comtesse de Leusse
     [mah-dmwah-zehl lah ko(n)-tehs duh luhz]
Mlle Madeleine de Vauzolles
     [mah-dmwah-zehl mah-dlehn duh vo-zol]
Mlle Marie Dauvesse
     [mah-dmwah-zehl mah-hree do-vehs]
Mlle Marie Drivon
     [mah-dmwah-zehl mah-hree dree-vo(n)]
Mlle Marie Gaze   [mah-dmwah-zehl mah-hree gahz]
Mlle Marthe Carron
     [mah-dmwah-zehl mahrt kah-hro(n)]

Mme A. Meilland	[mah-dahm A. may(h)-a(n)]
Mme A Meilland, Climbing	[mah-dahm A. may(h)-(y)a(n)]
Mme A. Labbey	[mah-dahm lah-bay]
Mme Abel Chatenay	[mah-dahm a-behl shah-tnay]
Mme Abel Chatenay, Climbing	[mah-dahm ah-behl shah-tnay]
Mme Alboni	[mah-dahm ahl-bo-nee]
Mme Alfred Carrière	[mah-dahm ahl-frehd kah-hryehr]
Mme Alfred de Rougemont	
	[mah-dahm ahl-fhrehd duh-hroo-zhmo(n)]
Mme Alice Garnier	[mah-dahm ah-lees gahr-nyay]
Mme Alphonse Seux	[mah-dahm ahl-fo(n)s suh]
Mme Ancelot	[mah-dahm a(n)-slo]
Mme Antoine Mari	[mah-dahm a(n)-twahn mah-hree]
Mme Antoine Meilland	
	[mah-dahm a(n)-twahn may(h)-(y)a(n)]
Mme Antoine Rébé	[mah-dahm a(n)-twahn hray-bay]
Mme Apolline Foulon	[mah-dahm ah-po-leen foo-lo(n)]
Mme Arthur Oger	[mah-dahm ahr-tewr o-zhay]
Mme Auguste Perrin	[mah-dahm o-gewst peh-rah(n)]
Mme Augustine Guinoisseau	
	[mah-dahm o-gews-teen gee-nwah-so]
Mme Bérard	[mah-dahm bay-hrahr]
Mme Berkeley	[mah-dahm]
Mme Boll	[mah-dahm bol]
Mme Bollinger	[mah-dahm]
Mme Bovary	[mah-dahm bo-vah-ree]
Mme Bravy	[mah-dahm brah-vee]
Mme Bréon	[mah-dahm bray-o(n)]
Mme Brosse	[mah-dahm bros]
Mme Camille	[mah-dahm kah-meey]
Mme Caroline Küster	[mah-dahm kah-hro-leen]
Mme Caroline Testout	[mah-dahm kah-hro-leen teh-too]
Mme Caroline Testout, Climbing	
	[mah-dahm kah-hro-leen teh-too]
Mme Cécile Brünner	[mah-dahm say-seel]
Mme Charles	[mah-dahm shahrl]
Mme Charles Baltet	[mah-dahm shahrl bahl-teh]
Mme Chevalier	[mah-dahm shuh-vah-lyay]
Mme Claude Olivier	[mah-dahm klod o-lee-vyay]
Mme Cochet-Cochet	[mah-dahm ko-sheh ko-sheh]

Mme Constans   [mah-dahm ko(n)s-ta(n)]
Mme Constant Soupert   [mah-dahm ko(n)s-ta(n) soo-pehr]
Mme Cordier   [mah-dahm kor-dyay]
Mme Cornélissen   [mah-dahm kohr-nay-lee-sa(n)]

Mme Couturier-Mention
                [mah-dahm koo-tew-ryay ma(n)-seeyo(n)]
Mme Crego   [mah-dahm kruh-go]
Mme Creux   [mah-dahm kruh]
Mme d'Arblay   [mah-dahm dahr-blay]
Mme d'Enfert   [mah-dahm da(n)-fehr]
Mme d'Hebray   [mah-dahm duh-bray]
Mme de Cambacérès
                [mah-dahm duh k[a]n-bah-say-hrehs]
Mme de Knorr   [mah-dahm duh knohr]
Mme de la Duchesse d'Auerstädt
                [mah-dahm duh lah dew-shehs]
Mme de la Rôche-Lambert
                [mah-dahm duh lah hrosh la(n)-bayhr]
Mme de Sancy de Parabère
                [mah-dahm duh sa(n)-see duh pah-hrah-behr]
Mme de Sertat   [mah-dahm duh sehr-tah]
Mme de Sévigné   [mah-dahm duh say-vee-neeyay]
Mme de Stella   [mah-dahm duh steh-lah]
Mme de Tartas   [mah-dahm duh tahr-tah]
Mme de Watteville   [mah-dahm duh vah-tveel]
Mme Delaroche-Lambert
                [mah-dahm duh-lah-rosh la(n)-behr]
Mme Delbard ®   [mah-dahm dehl-bahr]
Mme Denise Cassegrain   [mah-dahm duh-neez kahs-grah(n)]
Mme Denise Gallois   [mah-dahm duh-neez gah-lwah]
Mme Désirée Giraud   [mah-dahm day-zee-ray zhee-hro]
Mme Desprez   [mah-dahm day-pray]
Mme Dieudonné   [mah-dahm dyuh-do-nay]
Mme Doré   [mah-dahm do-hray]
Mme Dreout   [mah-dahm druh-oo]
Mme Driout   [mah-dahm dree-oo]
Mme Dubost   [mah-dahm dew-bo]
Mme Edmond Laporte   [mah-dahm ayd-mo(n) lah-port]
Mme Edmond Rostand   [mah-dahm ayd-mo(n) hros-ta(n)]

Mme Edouard Herriot   [mah-dahm ay-dwahr ay-hreeyo]
Mme Edouard Herriot, Climbing
                             [mah-dahm ay-dwahr ay-hreeyo]
Mme Edouart Ory   [mah-dahm ay-dwahr ohree]
Mme Eliza de Vilmorin
                  [mah-dahm ay-leezah duh veel-mo-rah(n)]
Mme Emile Seneclauze   [mah-dahm ay-meel suh-nuh-kloz]
Mme Emilie Charrin
                    [mah-dahm ay-mee-lee shah-hrah(n)]
Mme Emilie Charron
                    [mah-dahm ay-mee-lee shah-hro(n)]
Mme Ernest Calvat   [mah-dahm ehr-nehst kahl-vah]
Mme Ernest Levavasseur
                    [mah-dahm ehr-nehst luh-vah-vahsuhr]
Mme Ernest Piard   [mah-dahm ehr-nehst pyahr]
Mme Ernest Picard   [mah-dahm ehr-nehst pee-kahr]
Mme Eugene Marlitt   [mah-dahm uh-zhehn mahr-leet]
Mme Eugène Résal   [mah-dahm uh-zhehn hray-zahl]
Mme Falcot   [mah-dahm fahl-ko]
Mme Ferdinand Jamin
                  [mah-dahm fehr-dee-na(n) zhah-mah(n)]
Mme Fernandel ®   [mah-dahm fehr-na(n)-dehl]
Mme Fillion   [mah-dahm fee-leeyo(n)]
Mme Foureau   [mah-dahm foo-hro]
Mme Francois Pittet   [mah-dahm fra(n)-swah pee-teh]
Mme Gabriel Luizet
                    [mah-dahm gah-bree-yehl lwee-zeh]
Mme Georges Bruant   [mah-dahm zhohr-zh brew-a(n)]
Mme Georges Delbard ®   [mah-dahm zhor-zh dehl-bahr]
Mme Grégoire Staechelin
                    [mah-dahm gray-gwahr stah-shlah(n)]
Mme Gustave Bonner   [mah-dahm gews-tahv bo-nay]
Mme Hardy   [mah-dahm ahr-dee]
Mme Hébert   [mah-dahm ay-behr]
Mme Hector Leuillot   [mah-dahm ehk-tohr luh-leeyo]
Mme Hélène Parmentier
                    [mah-dahm ay-lehn pahr-ma(n)-tyay]
Mme Henri Fontaine
                    [mah-dahm a(n)-hree fo(n)-tehn]
Mme Henri Guillot   [mah-dahm a(n)-hree gee-yo]

Mme Henri Guillot, Climbing [mah-dahm a(n)-hree gee-yo]]
Mme Henri Queuille Gaujard [mah-dahm kuh-yuh go-zhar]
Mme Hermann Haefliger   [mah-dahm]
Mme Hide   [mah-dahm]
Mme Isaac Pereire   [mah-dahm ee-zahk puh-hrehr]
Mme J-P Soupert   [mah-dahm J-P soo-pehr]
Mme Jean Dupuy   [mah-dahm zha(n) dew-pwee]
Mme Jean Gaujard   [mah-dahm zhah(n) go-zhahr]
Mme Jeannine Joubert   [mah-dahm zhah-neen zhoo-behr]
Mme Jenny   [mah-dahm]
Mme Joseph Bonnaire   [mah-dahm zho-zehf bo-nehr]
Mme Joseph Perraud   [mah-dahm zho-zehf peh-hro]
Mme Joseph Schwartz   [mah-dahm zho-zehf]
Mme Jules Bouché   [mah-dahm zhewl boo-shay]
Mme Jules Bouche, Climbing [mah-dahm zhewl boosh]
Mme Jules Finger   [mah-dahm zhewl]
Mme Jules Francke   [mah-dahm zhewl]
Mme Jules Gravereaux   [mah-dahm zhewl grah-vro]
Mme Jules Grolez   [mah-dahm zhewl gro-lay]
Mme Jules Thibaud   [mah-dahm zhewl tee-bo]
Mme Julie Lasseu   [mah-dahm zhew-lee lah-suh]
Mme Juliette Guillot   [mah-dahm zhew-lyet gee-yo]
Mme Knorr   [mah-dahm knohr]
Mme Kriloff   [mad-dahm kree-lof]
Mme L. Dieudonné   [mah dam L. dyuh-do-nay]
Mme la Comtesse de Casserta
              [mah-dahm lah ko(n)-tehs duh kah-sehr-tah]
Mme la Duchesse d'Auerstadt [mah-dahm lah dew-shehs]
Mme la Général Paul de Benoist
              [mah-dahm lah gay-nay-rahl pol duh buh-nwah]
Mme Lambard   [mah-dahm la(n)-bahr]
Mme Landeau   [mah-dahm la(n)-do]
Mme Laurette Messimy   [mah-dahm lo-hreht meh-see-mee]
Mme Lauriol de Barny
                 [mah-dahm lo-hreeyol duh bahr-nee]
Mme Legras de Saint Germain
              [mah-dahm luh-grah duh sah(n) zhayhr-mah(n)]
Mme Léon Pain   [mah-dahm lay-o(n) pah(n)]
Mme Léonie Lamesch   [mah-dahm layo-nee lah-mehsh]

Mme Letuvée de Colnet
> [mah-dahm luh-tew-vay duh kol-neh]

Mme Lierval   [mah-dahm lyehr-vahl]
Mme Line Renaud   [mah-dahm leen hruh-no]
Mme Lombard   [mah-dahm lo(n)-bahr]
Mme Louis Armand   [mah-dahm loo-wee ahr-ma(n)]
Mme Louis Bernard   [mad-dahm loo-wee behr-nahr]
Mme Louis Laperrière
> [mah-dahm loo-wee lah-peh-hryehr]

Mme Louis Lévèque   [mah-dahm loo-wee lay-vehk]
Mme Louis Ricard   [mah-dahm loo-wee hree-kahr]
Mme Louise Piron   [mah-dahm loo-weez pee-hro(n)]
Mme Marie Curie   [mah-dahm mah-hree kew-hree]
Mme Maryna Auberville
> [mah-dahm mah-hree-nah o-behr-veel]

Mme Massot   [mah-dahm mah-so]
Mme Maurice Fenaile   [mah-dahm mo-hrees fuh-nahye]
Mme Maurin   [mah-dahm mo-hrah(n)]
Mme Mélanie Willermoz
> [mah-dahm may-lah-nee vee-lehr-moz]

Mme Moreau   [mah-dahm mo-hro]
Mme Moser   [mah-dahm mo-zay]
Mme Mossot   [mah-dahm mo-so]
Mme Neige   [mah-dahm nehzh]
Mme Nérard   [mah-dahm nay-hrahr]
Mme Nicolas Aussel   [mah-dahm nee-ko-lah o-sehl]
Mme Nobecourt   [mah-dahm no-buh-koohr]
Mme Norbert Levavasseur
> [mah-dahm nohr-behr luh-vah-vah-suhr]

Mme Paul Massad ®   [mah-dahm pol mah-sah]
Mme Paula Guisez   [mah-dahm gee-say]
Mme Philbert Boutigne
> [mah-dahm fee-lee-behr boo-teeney]

Mme Philippe Plantamour
> [mah-dahm fee-leep pla(n)-tah-moohr]

Mme Pierre Cochet   [mah-dahm pyehr ko-sheh]
Mme Pierre Euler   [mah-dahm pyehr uh-lay]
Mme Pierre Oger   [mah-dahm pyehr o-zhay]
Mme Pierre S. duPont   [mah-dahm pyehr S dew-po(n)]
Mme Plantier   [mah-dahm pla(n)-tyay]

Mme Platz   [mah-dahm plahtz]
Mme Prévost   [mah-dahm pray-vo]
Mme Ravary   [mah-dahm rah-vah-hree]
Mme Renahy   [mah-dahm hruh-nah-ee]
Mme René Coty   [mah-dahm hruh-nay ko-tee]
Mme Renée Gravereaux   [mah-dahm hruh-nay grah-vro]
Mme Rosa Monnet   [mah-dahm hro-zah mo-nay]
Mme Sancy de Parabère
                [mah-dahm sa(n)-see duh pah-hrah-behr]
Mme Scipion Cochet [Bernaix]
                [mah-dahm see-peeyo(n) ko-sheh] [behr-nay]
Mme Scipion Cochet [Cochet]
                [mah-dahm see-peeyo(n) ko-sheh] [ko sheh]
Mme Segond Weber   [mah-dahm suh-go(n) vay-behr]
Mme Segond Weber, Climbing [mah-dahm suh-go(n) vay-behr]
Mme Solvay   [mah-dahm sol-vay]
Mme Sophie Charlotte   [mah-dahm so-fee shahr-lot]
Mme Souchet   [mah-dahm soo-sheh]
Mme Soupert   [mah-dahm soo-pehr]
Mme Souveton   [mah-dahm soo-vto(n)]
Mme Speaker   [mah-dahm]
Mme Stolz   [mah-dahm]
Mme Taft   [mah-dahm]
Mme Teresa Esteban   [mah-dahm]
Mme Thiers   [mah-dahm tyehr]
Mme Trifle Levet   [mah-dahm treefl luh-veh]
Mme Tsiranana   [mah-dahm tsee-hrah-nah-nah]
Mme Victor Verdier   [mah-dahm veek-tohr vehr-dyay]
Mme Violet   [mah-dahm veeyo-leh]
Mme Wagram, Comtesse de Turenne
                [mah-dahm vah-grahm ko(n)-tehs duh tew-hrehn]
Mme William Paul   [mah-dahm wee-lyahm pol]
Mme Yvonne Chaverot   [mah-dahm ee-von shah-vro]
Mme Zoetmans   [mah-dahm]
Molineux ®   [mo-lee-nuh]
Mon Ami   [mo(n) ah-mee]
Mon Chéri ®   [mo(n) shay-hree]
Mon Jardin et Ma Maison ®
                [mo(n) zhahr-dah(n) ay mah may-zo(n)]
Mon Petit   [mo(n) puh-tee]

Mon Trésor	[mo(n) tray-zohr]
Mondiale	[mo(n)-dee-yahl]
Monet	[mo-neh]
Monique	[mo-neek]
Monsieur A. Maillé	[muh-syuh a. mah-yay]
Monsieur Boncenne	[muh-syuh bo(n)-sehn]
Monsieur Cordeau	[muh-syuh kohr-do]
Monsieur de Montigny	[muh-syuh duh mo(n)-teeneey]
Monsieur de Morand	[nuh-syuh duh mo-ra(n)]
Monsieur Désir	[muh-syuh day-zeer]
Monsieur Ernest Dupré	[muh-syuh ehr-nehst dew-pray]
Monsieur Georges de Cadoudal	
	[muh-syuh zhor-zh duh kah-doo-dahl]
Monsieur Gourdault	[muh-syuh goohr-do]
Monsieur Journeaux	[muh-syuh zhoohr-no]
Monsieur le Capitaine Louis Frère	
	[muh-syuh luh kah-pee-tehn loo-wee frehr]
Monsieur Louis Ricard	[muh-syuh loo-wee hree-kahr]
Monsieur Paul Ledé	[muh-syuh pol luh-day]
Monsieur Pélisson	[muh-syuh pay-lee-so(n)]
Monsieur Tillier	[muh-syuh tee-lyay]
Montauban	[mo(n)-to-ba(n)]
Montauban de Bretagne ®	
	[mo(n)-to-ba(n) duh bruh-tah-neey]
Montblanc	[mo(n)-bla(n)]
Montréal ®	[mo(n)-hray-ahl]
Montrésor	[mo(n)-tray-zohr]
Moulin Rouge ®	[moo-lah(n) hroozh]
Mousseau Ancien	[moo-so a(n)-syah(n)]
Mousseline	[moo-sleen]
Mousseux ancien	[moo-suh a(n)-syah(n)]
Mousseux du Japon	[moo-suh dew zhah-po(n)]
Moussue Partout	[moo-sew pahr-too]
Mrs G. Delbard	[dehl-bahr]
Mrs Pierre S. duPont	[pyehr S. dew-po(n)]
Mrs Pierre S. duPont, Climbing	
	[pyehr S. dew-po(n)]
Multiflore de Vaumarcus	
	[mewl-tee-flohr duh vo-mahr-kews]
Muriel	[mew-hryehl]

Mystelle	[mees-tehl]
Mystère	[mees-tehr]
Mystique	[mees-teek]
Naissance de Vénus	[nay-sa(n)s duh vay-news]
Nana Mouskouri	[nah-nah moos-koo-hree]
Napoléon	[nah-po-lay-o(n)]
Narcisse de Salvande	[nahr-sees duh sahl-va(n)d]
Neige d'Avril	[nehzh dah-vreel]
Neige d'Eté ®	[nehzh day-tay]
Neige Parfum	[nehzh pahr-fah(n)]
Neige Rose	[nehzh hroz]
Neron	[nuh-hro(n)]
Nestor	[nehs-tohr]
New Rouge Meilland	[hroozh may(h)-a(n)]
Nicole ®	[nee-kol]
Nicolette	[nee-ko-leht]
Nigrette	[nee-greht]
Nil Bleu ®	[neel bluh]
Niles Cochet	[ko-sheh]
Niphetos	[neef-tos]
Niphetos, Climbing	[neef-tos]
Nitouche ®	[nee-toosh]
Noblesse TM	[no-blehs]
Noëlla Nabonnand	[no-ehlah na-bo-na(n)]
Noëlle Marie	[no-ehl mah-hree]
Noisette Desprez	[nwah-zeht day-pray]
Noisette Garden Pink Tea	[nwah-zeht]
Noisette Rose	[nwah-zeht hroz]
Normandie	[nohr-ma(n)-dee]
Notre Dame	[notr dahm]
Notre Père	[notr pehr]
Nouveau Monde	[noo-vo mo(n)d]
Nouveau Rouge	[noo-vo hroozh]
Nouveau Vulcain	[noo-vo vewl-kah(n)]
Nouvelle Europe	[noo-vehl uh-hrop]
Nouvelle Pivoine	[noo-vehl pee-vwahn]
Nouvelle Transparente	[noo-vehl tra(n)s-pah-ra(n)t]
Nuage Blanc ®	[new-ahzh bla(n)]
Nuage Parfumé ®	[new-ahzh pahr-few-may]
Nuage Parfume, Climbing	[new-ahzh pahr-few-may]

Nubienne	[new-byehn]
Nuit d'Orient ®	[nwee dohr-eeya(n)]
Nuit de Velours	[nwee duh vuh-loohr]
Nuit de Young	[nwee duh]
Nymphe Egéria	[nah(n)f ay-gay-hryah]
Nymphe Tépla	[nah(n)f tay-plah]
Odyssée ®	[o-dee-say]
Œillet Flamand	[uh-yay flah-ma(n)]
Œillet Panachée	[uh-yay pah-nah-shay]
Œillet Parfait	[uh-yay pahr-fay]
Oh La La	[o lah lah]
Olala	[o-lah-lah]
Ombrée Parfaite	[o(n)-bray pahr-fayt]
Orage d'Été ®	[o-hrahzh day-tay]
Orange Château	[o-hra(n)zh shah-to]
Orange Sauvageot	[o-hra(n)zh so-vah-zho]
Orange Vilmorin	[o-hra(n)zh veel-mo-hrah(n)]
Orangeade	[o-hra(n)-zhahd]
Orléans Rose	[ohr-lay-a(n) hroz]
Ornement de la Nature	[ohr-nuh-ma(n) duh lah nah-tewr]
Ornement des Bosquets	[ohr-nuh-ma(n) day bos-keh]
Orpheline de Juillet	[ohr-fuh-leen duh zhwee-yay]

Rose Notes:

Rose panachée de Bordeaux.

Panachée de Bourdeaux

[pah-nah-shay duh bohr-do]

PQR French

Palissade Rose ®	[pah-lee-sahd hroz]
Panachée à Fleurs Doubles	[pah-nah-shay ah fluhr doobl]
Panachée à Fleurs Pleines	[pah-nah-shay ah fluhr plehn]
Panachée d'Angers	[pah-nah-shay da(n)-zhay]
Panachée d'Orléans	[pah-nah-shay dohr-lay-a(n)]
Panachée de Bordeaux	[pah-nah-shay duh bohr-do]
Panachée de Lyon	[pah-nah-shay duh lee-yo(n)]
Panachée Double	[pah-nah-shay doobl]
Panachée Superbe	[pah-nah-shay sew-pehrb]
Panorama	[pah-no-rah-mah]
Panthère Rose	[pa(n)-tehr hroz]
Papa Gontier	[pah-pah go(n)-tyay]
Papa Gontier, Climbing	[pah-pah go(n)-tyay]
Papa Hémeray	[pah-pah ay-mray]
Papa Meilland ®	[pah-pah may(h)-(y)a(n)]
Papa Meilland, ® Climbing	[pah-pah may(h)-(y)a(n)]
Papi Delbard ®	[pah-pee dehl-bahr]
Papillon [Dubourg]	[pah-pee-yo(n) [dew-boohr]]
Papillon [Nabonnand]	[pah-pee-yo(n) [nah-bo-na(n)]]
Pâquerette	[pahk-rhet]
Parapluie de Neige	[pah-rah-plwee dun nehzh]
Parfait	[pahr-fay]
Parfum d'Armor ®	[pahr-fah(n) dahr-mohr]
Parfum d'Ispahan	[pahr-fah(n) dees-pah-a(n)]
Parfum de Franche-Comté ®	
	[pahr-fah(n) duh fra(n)sh ko(n)-tay]
Parfum de l'Haÿ	[pahr-fah(n) duh lah-ee]

Parfum Liffreen	[pahr-fah(n)
Parfum Rose ®	[pahr-fah(n) hroz]
Paris	[pah-hree]
Paris de Yves St Laurent TM	
	[pah-hree duh eev sah(n) lo-hra(n)]
Paris Pink	[pah-hree]
Pariser Charme ®	[pah-hree-zay shahrm]
Parmentier	[pahr-ma(n)-tyay]
Parure d'Or ®	[pah-hrewr dohr]
Pas de Deux	[pah duh duh]
Pasteur	[pahs-tuhr]
Patte de Velours ®	[paht duh vuh-loohr]
Paul Bocuse TM	[pol bo-kewz]
Paul Cezanne ®	[pol seh-zahn]
Paul Dauvesse	[pol do-vehs]
Paul de Fontaine	[pol duh fo(n)-tehn]
Paul de la Maillery	[pol duh lah may(h)-yuh-hree]
Paul de la Meilleraye	[pol duh lah may(h)-yuh-hray]
Paul Gauguin ®	[pol go-gah(n)]
Paul Jamain	[pol zhah-mah(n)]
Paul Lédé, Climbing	[pol lay-day]
Paul Nabonnand	[pol nah-bo-na(n)]
Paul Neyron	[pol nay-ro(n)]
Paul Noël	[pol noehl]
Paul Perras	[pol peh-rah]
Paul Ricard ®	[pol hree-kahr]
Paul Ricault	[pol hree-ko]
Paul Richard	[pol hree-shahr]
Paul Shirville	[pol]
Paul Transon	[pol tra(n)-so(n)]
Paul Verdier	[pol vehr-dyay]
Paulette	[po-leht]
Pauline Bonaparte	[po-leen bo-nah-pahrt]
Pavillon de Prégny	[pah-vee-yo(n) duh pray-neey]
Peaudouce	[po-doos]
Pêche Meillandina ®	[pehsh may(h)-(y)a[n-dee-nah]
Pélisson	[pay-lee-so(n)]
Perfection de Monplaisir	
	[pehr-fehk-seeyo(n) duh mo(n)-play-zeer]
Pergolèse	[pehr-go-lehz]

Princesse de Vaudemont   [prah(n) sehs duh vod-mo(n)]
Princesse de Venosa   [prah(n)-sehs duh]
Princesse Étienne de Croy   [prah(n)-sehs ay-tyehn duh krwah]
Princesse Joséphine-Charolette
                                 [prah(n)-sehs zho-zay-feen shah-hro-leht]
Princesse Grâce   [prah(n)-sehs grahs]
Princesse Grâce de Monaco
                                 [prah(n)-sehs grahs duh mo-nah-ko]
Princesse Lamballe   [prah(n)-sehs la(n)-bahl]
Princesse Louise   [prah(n)-sehs loo-weez]
Princesse Margaret d'Angleterre
                                 [prah(n)-sehs da(n)-gluh-tehr]
Princesse Marie   [prah(n)-sehs mah-hree]
Princesse Marie Adélaïde de Luxembourg
   [prah(n)-sehs mah-hree ah-day-lah-eed duh lewk-sa(n)-boohr]
Privé   [pree-vay]
Professeur Christian Cabrol   [pro-feh-suhr krees-tya(n) kah-brol]
Professeur Émile Perrot   [pro-feh-suhr ay-meel peh-hro]
Professeur Ganiviat   [pro-feh-suhr gah-nee-vyah]
Professeur Jean Barnard   [pro-feh-suhr zha(n) bahr-nahr]
Prolifera de Redoute   [pro-lee-fay-rah duh ruh-doot]
Prominent ®   [pro-mee-na(n)]
Provence ®   [pro-va(n)s]
Provence Bersoe   [pro-va(n)s]]
Provence d'Anjou   [pro-va(n)s da(n)-zhoo]
Provence Panachée   [pro-va(n)s pah-nah-shay]
Provence Rose   [pro-va(n)s hroz]
Provins Renoncule   [pro-vah(n) ruh-no(n)-kewl]
Pucelle de Lille   [pew-sehl duh leel]
Puy du Fou ®   [pwee dew foo]
Pyrénées   [pee-hray-nay]
Quatre Saisons   [kahtr say-zo(n)]
Quatre Saisons Blanc Mousseux
                                 [kahtr say-zo(n) bla(n) moo-suh]
Quatre Saisons d'Italie   [kahtr say-zo(n) dee-tah-lee]
Quatre Saisons Royale   [kahtr say-zo(n) rwah-yahl]
Québec   [kay-behk]
Rabelais ®   [hrah-blay]
Radox Bouquet   [hra-doks boo-keh]
Raymond Chenault   [hray-mo(n) shuh-no]

Red Cécile Brunner	[say-seel]
Red Fleurette	[fluh-rhet]
Red Garnette	[gahr-neht]
Red Maman Cochet	[mah-ma(n) ko-sheh]
Red Meidiland ®	[may-dee-la(n)]
Red Meillandina ®	[may(h)-(y)a[n-dee-nah]
Red Orléans Rose	[ohr-lay-a(n) hroz]
Red Parfum ®	[pahr-fah(n)
Red Provence	[pro-va(n)s]
Red Rosette	[hro-zeht]
Red Roulette	[hroo-leht]
Redouté	[hruh-doo-tay]
Régine Crespin ®	[hray-zheen kreh-pah(n)]
Reine Blanche [Lee]	[hrehn bla(n)sh] [lee]
Reine Blanche [Robert]	[hrehn bla(n)sh] [hro-behr]
Reine Chabeau ®	[hrhehn shab-bo]
Reine d'Espagne	[hrhehn dehs-pahneey]
Reine de I'll de Bourbon	[hrehn duh leel duh boohr-bo(n)
Reine de Perse	[hrehn duh pehrs]
Reine de Prusse	[hrehn duh prews]
Reine de Saxe	[hrehn duh sahks]
Reine des Amateurs	[hrehn day ah-mah-tuhr]
Reine des Belges	[hrehn day behlzh]
Reine des Bordures	[hrehn day bohr-dewr]
Reine des Centfeuilles	[hrehn day sa(n)-fuh-yuh]
Reine des Français	[hrehn day fra(n)-say]
Reine des Iles bourbon	[hrehn day zeel boohr-bo(n)]
Reine des Mousseuses	[hrehn day moo-suhz]
Reine des Moussues	[hrehn day moo-sew]
Reine des Neiges	[hrehn day nehzh]
Reine des Neiges, Climbing	[rhrehn day nehzh]
Reine des Roses	[hrehn day hroz]
Reine des Vierges	[hrehn day vyehr-zh]
Reine des Violettes	[hrehn day veeyo-layt]
Reine du Danemark	[hrehn dew dah-nmahrk]
Reine du Forez	[hrehn dew fo-hray]
Reine du Midi	[hrehn dew mee-dee]
Reine France	[hrehn fra(n)s]
Reine Lucia	[hrehn lew-syah]
Reine Marguerite d'Italie	[hrehn mahr-guh-hreet dee-tah-lee]

Reine Marie Henriette	[hrehn mah-hree a(n)-hryet]
Reine Olga de Wurtemberg	[hrehn ol-gah duh]
Relax Meidiland ®	[meh-dee-la(n)]
Relax Meillandécor ®	[may(h)-(y)a(n)-day-kohr]
Rémy Martin	[hray-mee mahr-tah(n)]
Renaissance [Gaujard]	[hruh-nay-sa(n)s] [go-zhahr]]
Rendez-vous ®	[hra(n)-day voo]
René André	[hruh-nay a(n)-dray]
René d'Anjou	[hruh-nay da(n)-zhoo]
Renée Danielle	[hruhneh dah-nyehl]
Renoncule	[hruh-no(n)-kewl]
Repens Alba	[hruh-pa(n) ahl-bah]
Repens Meidiland	[hruh-pa(n) may-dee-la(n)]
République de Geneva ®	
	[hray-pew-bleek duh zhuh-neh-vah]
Rétro ®	[hray-tro]
Rêve d'Or	[hrehv dohr]
Rêve d'un Soir	[hreev dah(n) swahr]
Rêve de Deauville	[hrehv duh do-veel]
Rêve de Paris ®	[hrehv duh pah-hree]
Réveil	[hray-vay(h)]
Réveil Dijonnais	[hray-vay(h) dee-zho-nay]
Révérend H. d'Ombrain	[hray-vay-hra(n) H. do(n)-brah(n)]
Rêverie ®	[hreh-vree]
Révolution Francaise ®	[hray-vo-lew-syo(n) fra(n)-sehz]
Revue ®	[hruh-vew]
Rhodoloque Jules Gravereaux	[hro-do-lok zhewl grah-vro]
Rina Hugo	[ree-nah ew-go]
Risque	[hreesk]
Rival de Paestrum	[ree-vahl duh]
Rivière de Diamant ®	[hree-vyehr duh dyah-ma(n)]
Robe de Neige ®	[hrob duh nehzh]
Robe de Soie ®	[hrob duh swah]
Robe Fleurie ®	[hrob fluh-hree]
Robert le Diable	[hro-behr luh deeyah-bl]
Robert Léopold	[hro-behr lay-opol]
Robinette	[hro-bee-neht]
Roger Lambelin	[hro-zhay la(n)-buh-lah(n)]
Roi de Pays-Bas	[hrwah day payee bah]
Roi de Siam	[hrwah duh seeyahm]

Roi des Aunes	[hrwah day on]
Roi des Bordures	[hrwah day bohr-dewr]
Roi des Pourpres	[hrwah day poohrpr]
Romarin	[hro-mah-rah(n)]
Rose à feuilles de chanvre	[hroz ah fuh-yuh duh sha(n)vr]
Rose à Feuilles de Laitue	[hroz ah fuh-yuh duh lay-tew]
Rose à fleurs gigantesques	[hroz ah fluhr zhee-ga(n)-tehsk]
Rose à fruitis d'Ornement	
	[hroz ah frwee-tees dohr-nuh-ma(n)]
Rose à longs Pédoncules	[hroz ah lo(n) pay-do(n)-kewl]
Rose à Parfum de Grasse	[hroz ah pahr-fah(n) duh grahs]
Rose à Parfum de l'Haÿ	[hroz ah pahr-fah(n) duh lah-ee]
Rose Arthur Goodwin et Willowmere	
	[hroz ahr-tewr]
Rose Besson	[hroz beh-so(n)]
Rose Blanche	[hroz bla(n)sh]
Rose Cascade ®	[hroz kahs-kahd]
Rose Céleste ®	[hroz say-lehst]
Rose Chou	[hroz shoo]
Rose Chou de Hollande	[hroz shoo duh o-la(n)d]
Rose d'Amour	[hroz dah-moohr]
Rose d'Annecy ®	[hroz dahn-see]
Rose d'Hivers	[hroz dee-vayhr]
Rose d'Isfahan	[hroz dees-faha(n)]
Rose d'Or de Montreaux ®	[hroz dohr duh mo(n)-tro]
Rose d'Orsay	[hroz dohr-say]
Rose de Bangale	[hroz duh ba(n)-gahl]
Rose de Castile	[hroz duh kahs-teey]
Rose de l'Isle	[hroz duh leel]
Rose de la Maitre Ecole	[hroz duh lah mehtr ay-kol]
Rose de la Reine	[hroz duh lah hrehn]
Rose de Loire	[hroz duh lah lwahr]
Rose de Mai	[hroz duh may]
Rose de Meaux	[hroz duh mo]
Rose de Meaux Blanc	[hroz duh mo bla(n)]
Rose de Montfort ®	[hroz duh mo(n)-fohr]
Rose de Plaquer	[hroz duh plah-kay]
Rose de Provins	[hroz duh pro-vah(n)]
Rose de Puteaux	[hroz duh pew-to]
Rose de Rennes ®	[hroz duh rehn]

Rose de Rescht   [hroz]
Rose des Cisterciens ®   [hroz day sees-tehr-syah(n)]
Rose des Maures   [hroz day mohr]
Rose des Peintres   [hroz day pah(n)tr]
Rose du Maître d'École   [hroz dew maytr day-kol]
Rose du Roi   [hroz dew hrwah]
Rose du Roi à Fleurs Pourpres
                                        [hroz dew hrwah ah fluhr poohr-pr]
Rose du Roi Panachée
                                        [hroz dew hrwah pah-nah-shay]
Rose du Saint-Sacrement   [hroz dew sah(n) sah-kruh-ma(n)]
Rose Dubreuil   [hroz dew-bruh-yuh]
Rose Édouard   [hroz ay-dooahr]
Rose Gaujard ®   [hroz go-zhahr]
Rose Gaujard, ® Climbing ®   [hroz go-zhahr]
Rose Lyon   [hroz leeyo(n)]
Rose Marie, Climbing   [hroz mah-hree]
Rose Marie Viaud   [hruz mah-hree vee-yo]
Rose-Marie Viaud   [hroz mah-hree vee-yo]
Rose Meillandécor ®   [hroz [may(h)-(y)a(n) deh-kohr]
Rose Nabonnand   [hroz nah-bo-na(n)]
Rose Œillet de Saint Arquey Vilfray
                                        [hroz uh-yay duh sah(n) ahr-kay veel-fray]
Rose Pavot   [hroz pah-vo]
Rose Vert   [hroz vehr]
Rosée du Matin   [hro-zay dew mah-tah(n)]
Roseline de Kersaint ®   [hro-zuh-leen duh kehr-sah(n)]
Roseraie de Blois ®   [hroz-hray duh blwah]
Roseraie de l'Haÿ   [hro-zhray duh lah-ee]
Roseraie du Chatelet ®   [hroz-hray dew shah-tleh]
Rosette Delizy   [hro-zeht duh-lee-zee]
Rosier de la Malmaison
                                        [hro-syay duh lah mahl-may-zo(n)]
Rosier de Thionville   [hro-zyay duh tee-yo(n)-veel]
Rouge Adam ®   [hroozh ah-da(n)]
Rouge Admirable   [hroozh ahd-mee-hrahbl]
Rouge Éblouissante   [hroozh ay-bloo-eesa(n)t]
Rouge et Or ®   [hroozh ay ohr]
Rouge Koster   [hroozh]
Rouge Marbrée   [hroozh mahr-bray]

Rouge Meilland ®   [hroozh may(h)-(y)a(n)]
Rouge Meilland [Meilland, 1949]
                                    [hroozh may(h)- (y)a(n)]
Rouge Meilland [Meilland, 1982]
                                    [hroozh may(h)- (y)a(n)]
Rouge Meillandécor ®   [hroozh may(h)-(y)a(n)-day-kohr]
Rouge   [hroozh]
Rouge Moss   [hroozh]
Rouge Prolific   [hroozh]
Royal Marbrée   [rwah-yahl mahr-bray]

Rose Notes:

Rose Triomphe de Margottin

Triomphe de Margottin
[tree-yo(n)f duh mahr-go-tah(n)]

ST FRENCH

Sachet TM	[sah-sheh]
Saint-Émilion ®	[sah]n] tay-mee-leeyo(n)]
Saint-Exupéry	[sah(n) tehk-zew-pay-ree]
Saint-Fiacre d'Orléans	[sah(n) fyahkr dohr-lay-a(n)]
Saint Prist de Breuze	[sah(n) preest duh bruhz]
Salet	[sah-leh]
Salut à la Suisse	[sah-lew ah lah swees]
Salut d'Aix la chapelle	[sah-lew dehks lah shah-pehl]
Sanglant	[sa(n)-gla(n)]
Sanguine	[sa(n)-geen]
Sans Sepales	[sa(n) suh-pahl]
Sans Sepals	[sa(n) suh-pahl]
Sans Souci ® [Barni]	[sa(n) soo-see] [bahr-nee]
Sans Souci [Meilland]	[sa(n) soo-see] [may(h)-a(n)]
Saphir	[sah-feer]
Saramouche ®	[sah-rah-moosh]
Savoy Hôtel	[sa-vwah o-tehl]
Scarlet Meidiland ®	[meh-dee-la(n)]
Scarlet Meillandécor ®	[may(h)-(y)a(n)-day-kohr]
Sénat Romain	[say-nah hro-mah(n)]
Sénateur Amic	[say-nah-tuhr ah-meek]
Sénateur Lafollette	[say-nah-tuhr lah-fo-leht]
Sénateur Romain	[say-nah-tuhr ro-mah(n)]
Sénateur Vaisse	[say-nah-tuhr vehs]
Sénégal	[say-nay-ghal]
Sensass Delbard ®	[dehl-bahr]
Senteur des îles ®	[sa(n)-tuhr day zeel]

Senteur Royale ®	[sa(n)-tuhr rwah-yahl]
Sérénade	[say-ray-nahd]
Serène Bouquet TM	[suh-rehn boo-keh]
Sérénité ®	[say-ray-nee-tay]
Serpent Vert	[sehr-pa(n) vehr]
Sidonie	[see-do-nee]
Silhouette ®	[see-loo-eht]
Sissi ®	[see-see]
Soeur Marthe	[suhr mahrt]
Soeur Thérèse	[suhr tay-rehz]
Soir de Fête	[swahr duh feht]
Soirée de Bonheur ®	[swah-hray duh bo-nuhr]]
Soleil d'Angers	[so-lay(h) da(n)-zhay]
Soleil d'été ®	[so-lay(h) day-tay]
Soleil d'Or	[so-lay(h) dohr]
Soleil Rouge ®	[so-lay(h) hroozh]
Solfaterre	[sol-fah-tehr]
Solitaire ®	[so-lee-tehr]
Solitude TM	[so-lee-tewd]
Sombreuil	[so(n)-bruh-yuh]
Sonia	[so-neeya]
Sonia Meilland	[so-neeyah may(h)- (y)a(n)]
Sophie de Marsilly	[so-fee duh mahr-seeyee]
Sorbet ®	[sohr-bay]
Sorbet Bouquet	[sohr-bay boo-keh]
Sorbet Framboise ®	[sohr-bay fra(n)-bwahz]
Sorbet Fruité ®	[sohr-bay frwee-tay]
Soupert et Notting	[soo-pehr ay]
Sourire d'Antan ®	[soo-hreer da(n)-ta(n)]
Sourire d'Enfant ®	[soo-hreer da(n)-fa(n)]
Sourire d'Orchidée	[soo-hreer dohr-kee-day]
Sourire Rosel	[soo-hreer hro-zehl]
Souvenir d'Adèle Launay	[soo-vneer dah-dehl lo-nay]

Souvenir d'Adolphe de Charvoik

[soo-vneer dah-dolf duh shahr-vwahk]

Souvenir d'Adolphe Turc	[soo-vneer dah-dolf tewrk]

Souvenir d'Aimée Terrel des Chênes

[soo-vneer deh-may teh-rehl day shehn]

Souvenir d'Alaine Fontaine	[soo-vneer dah-lehn fo(n)-tehn]
Souvenir d'Alma de l'Aigle	[soo-vneer dahl-mah duh lehgl]

Souvenir d'Alphonse Lavallée   [soo-vneer dahl-fo(n)s lah-vah-lay]
Souvenir d'Auguste Legros   [soo-vneer do-gewst luh-gro]
Souvenir d'Élisa Vardon   [soo-vneer day-lee-zah vahr-do(n)]
Souvenir d'Élise   [soo-vneer day-leez]
Souvenir d'un Ami   [soo-vneer dah(n) nah-mee]
Souvenir d'un ami candidat
              [soo-vneer dah(n) ah-mee ka(n)-dee-dah]
Souvenir de Bernadin St Pierre
              [soo-vneer duh behr-nahr-dah(n) sah(n) pyehr]
Souvenir de Brod   [soo-vneer duh bro]
Souvenir de Christophe Cochet
              [soo-vneer duh krees-tof ko-sheh]
Souvenir de Claudius Denoyel
              [soo-vneer duh klo-dee-ews duh-nwah-yehl]
Souvenir de Claudius Pernet
              [soo-vneer duh klo-dyews pehr-neh]
Souvenir de Francois Gaulain
              [soo-vneer duh fra(n)-swah go-lah(n)]
Souvenir de Georges Pernet   [soo-vneer duh zhor-zh pehr-neh]
Souvenir de Germain St-Pierre
              [soo-vneer duh zhehr-mah(n) sah(n) pyehr]
Souvenir de Gilbert Nabonnand
              [soo-vneer duh zheel-behr nah-bo-na(n)]
Souvenir de Graton   [soo-vneer duh grah-to(n)]
Souvenir de Guillot   [soo-vneer duh gee-yo]
Souvenir de HA Verschuren   [soo-vneer duh]
Souvenir de J Chabert   [soo-vneer duh J. sha-behr]
Souvenir de J Mermet   [soo-vneer duh J.. mehr-meh]
Souvenir de Jeanne Balandreau
              [soo-vneer duh zhahn bah-la(n)-dro]
Souvenir de l'Impératrice Joséphine
          [soo-vneer duh lah(n)-pay-hrah-trees zho-zay-feen]
Souvenir de la Bataille de Marengo
          [soo-vneer duh lah..bah-tahye..duh mah-hra(n)-go]
Souvenir de la Malmaison
              [soo-vneer duh lah mahl-may-zo(n)]
Souvenir de la Malmaison, Climbing
              [soo-vneer duh lah mahl-may-zo(n)]
Souvenir de la Malmaison Rose
              [soo-vneer duh lah mahl-may-zo(n) hroz]

Souvenir de la Malmaison, Rouge
    [soo-vneer duh lah mahl-may-zo(n) hroozh
Souvenir de la Princesse de Lamballe
    [soo-vneer duh lah prah(n)-sehs duh la(n)-bahl]
Souvenir de la Reine d'Angleterre
    [soo-vneer duh lah hrehn da(n)-gluh-tehr]
Souvenir de Louis Amade ®   [soo-vneer duh loo-wee ah-mahd]
Souvenir de Lucie   [soo-vneer duh lew-see]
Souvenir de Malmedy   [soo-vneer duh]
Souvenir de McKinley   [soo-vneer duh]
Souvenir de Mlle Juliet de Bricard
   [soo-vneer duh mahd-mwah-zehl zhew-lyet duh bree-kahr]
Souvenir de Mme Auguste Charles
            [soo-vneer duh mah-dahm o-gewst shahrl]
Souvenir de Mme Berthier
              [soo-vneer duh mah-dahm behr-tyay]
Souvenir de Mme Boll   [soo-vneer duh mah-dahm bol]
Souvenir de Mme Boullet
             [soo-vneer duh mah-dahm boo-leh]
Souvenir de Mme Boullet, Climbing
            [soo-vneer duh mah-dahm boo-leh]
Souvenir de Mme Breuil
            [soo-vneer duh mah-dahm bruh-yuh]
Souvenir de Mme Breville
           [soo-vneer duh mah-dahm bruh-veey]
Souvenir de Mme Bruel
            [soo-vneer duh mah-dahm brew-ehl]
Souvenir de Mme de Corval
           [soo-vneer duh mah-dahm duh kohr-vahl]
Souvenir de Mme H. Thuret
            [soo-vneer duh mah-dahm H. tew-reh]

Souvenir de Mme Jeanne Balandreau
       [soo-vneer duh mah-dahm zhahn bah-la(n)-dro]
Souvenir de Mme Ladvocat
          [soo-vneer duh mah-dahm lahd-vo-kah]
Souvenir de Mme Léonie Viennot
        [soo-vneer duh mah-dahm layo-nee vyehn-no]
Souvenir de Mme Louise Crette
          [soo-vneer duh mah-dahm loo-weez kreht]

Souvenir de Mme Sablayrolles
    [soo-vneer duh mah-dahm sah-blay-hrol]
Souvenir de Némours   [soo-vneer duh nay-moor]
Souvenir de Paul Dupuy   [soo-vneer duh pol dew-pwee]
Souvenir de Philémon Cochet
    [soo-vneer duh fee-lay-mo(n) ko-sheh]
Souvenir de Pierre Dupuy   [soo-vneer duh pyehr dew-pwee]
Souvenir de Pierre Guillot   [soo-vneer duh pyehr gee-yo]
Souvenir de Pierre Notting   [soo-vneer duh pyehr]
Souvenir de Pierre Sionville
    [soo-vneer duh pyehr seeyo(n)-veel]
Souvenir de Pierre Vibert   [soo-vneer duh pyehr vee-behr]
Souvenir de Rose-Marie ®   [soo-vneer duh hroz mah-hree]
Souvenir de St Anne   [soo-vneer duh sah(n) ahn]
Souvenir de Thérèse Levet   [soo-vneer duh tay-hrehz luh-veh]
Souvenir de Victor Hugo   [soo-vneer duh veek-tohr ew-go]
Souvenir de Victor Landeau   [soo-vneer duh veek-tor la(n)-do]
Souvenir de Yeddo   [soo-vneer duh]
Souvenir du Docteur Jamain
    [soo-vneer duh dok-tuhr zhah-mah(n)]
Souvenir du Lieutenant Bujon
    [soo-vneer dew lyuh-tna(n) bew-zho(n)]
Souvenir du Président Carnot
    [soo-vneer dew pray-zee-da(n) kahr-no]
Souvenir du Président Lincoln   [soo-vneer dew pray-zee-da(n)]
Souvenir du Rosieriste Rambaux
    [soo-vneer dew hro-zyay-hreest ra(n)-bo]
Souvenirs de Marcel Proust ®   [soo-vneer duh mahr-sehl proost]
Souviens-Toi   [soo-vyah(n) twah]
Ste Thérèse de Lisieux   [sah(n)t tay-hrehz duh lee-zyuh]
Stéphanie de Monaco ®   [stay-fah-nee duh mo-nah-ko]
Stéphanie Diane   [stay-fah-nee dee-yahn]
Sultane   [sewl-tahn]
Surpasse tout   [sewr-pahs too]
Sympathie ®   [sah(n)-pah-tee]
Tamara   [tah-mah-rah]
Tambourine   [ta(n)-boo-reen]
Tapis d'Orient   [tah-pee doh-reeya(n)]
Tapis de Soie   [tah-pee duh swah]
Tapis Jaune   [tah-pee zhon]

Tapis Magique ®	[tah-pee mah-zheek]
Tapis Persan	[tah-pee pehr-sa(n)]
Tapis Rouge ®	[tah-pee hroozh]
Tapis Volant ®	[tah-pee vo-la(n)]
Tassin	[tah-sah(n)]
Tendresse ®	[ta(n)-drehs]
Thérèse Bauer	[tay-rehz]
Thérèse Bugnet	[tay-rehz bew-neeyeh]
Thérèse de Lisieux ®	[tay-rehz duh lee-zyuh]
Tipo Idéale	[tee-po ee-day-ahl]
Toison d'Or	[twah-zo(n) dohr]
Toque Rouge ®	[tok roozh]
Toulouse-Lautrec ®	[too-looz lo-trehk]
Tour de Malakoff	[toohr duh mah-lah-kof]
Tour Eiffel	[toohr eh-fehl]
Tourbillon	[toohr-beeyo(n)]
Tourmaline ®	[toohr-mah-leen]
Traverser	[trah-vayhr-say]
Travesti	[trah-vehs.tee]
Tricolore	[tree-ko-lohr]
Tricolore de Flandre	[tree-ko-lohr duh fla(n)dr]
Trier ®	[tryay]
Triolet	[treeyo-leh]
Triomphe Angevin	[tree-yo(n)f a(n)-zhvah(n)]
Triomphe d'Alencon	[tree-yo(n)f dah-la(n)-so(n)]
Triomphe d'Amiens	[tree-yo(n)f dah-meeah(n)]
Triomphe de Caen	[tree-yo(n)f duh ka(n)]
Triomphe de Flore	[tree-yo(n)f duh flohr]
Triomphe de France	[tree-yo(n)f duh fra(n)s]
Triomphe de Guillot	[tree-yo(n)f duh gee-yo]
Triomphe de l'Exposition	
	[tree-yo(n)f duh lehk-spo-zee-seeyo(n)]
Triomphe de la Guillotière	[tree-yo(n)f duh lah gee-yo-tyehr]
Triomphe de Laffay	[tree-yo(n)f duh lah-fay]
Triomphe de Luxembourg	[tree-yo(n)f duh lewk-sa(n)-boohr]
Triomphe de Margottin	[tree-yo(n)f duh mahr-go-tah(n)]
Triomphe des Noisettes	[tree-yo(n)f day nwah-zeht]
Triomphe du Luxembourg	[tree-yo(n)f dew lewk-sa(n)-boohr]
Triomphe Orléans	[tree-yo(n)f ohr-lay-a(n)]
Turbo Meidiland TM	[tewr-bo meh-dee-la(n)]

Tutu Mauve   [tew-tew mov]
Tzigane   [tsee-gahn]

Rosier à fruits d'ornement
Rosa macrophylla rugosa

Rosier à fruitis d'Ornement
[hro-syay frwee-tees dohr-nuh-ma(n)]

U-Z FRENCH

Unique Blanche	[ew-neek bla(n)sh]
Unique Blanche de Panachée	
	[ew-neek bla(n)sh duh pah-nah-shay]
Unique Blanche Panachée	
	[ew-neek bla(n)sh pah-nah-shay]
Unique Panachée	[ew-neek pah-nah-shay]
Unique Panachée [Caron]	
	[ew-neek pah-nah-shay] [Kah-ro(n)]
Unique Panachée [Pradel]	
	[ew-neek pah-nah-shay] [prah-dehl]
Unique Panachée Superbe	[ew-neek pah-nah-shay sew-pehrb]
Vaire	[vehr]
Val d'Authion	[vahl do-seeyo(n)]
Valenciennes	[vah-la(n)-syehn]
Vanille-Groseille ®	[vah-neey gro-zay(h)]
Varlon	[vahr-lo(n)]
Velay-Rose	[vuh-lay hroz]
Velours épiscopal	[vuh-loohr ay-pees-ko-pahl]
Velours Parfumé ®	[vuh-loohr pahr-few-may]
Velours Pourpre	[vuh-loohr poohrpr]
Velouté d'Orléans	[vuh-loohr dohr-lay-a(n)]
Vent d'été ®	[va(n) day-tay]
Vercors	[vehr-kohr]
Verdun	[vehr-dah(n)]
Vermillion Patio	[vehr-meeyo(n) pah-tyo]
Véronique	[vay-hro-neek]
Versailles ®	[vehr-sahye]

Versailles Palace ®	[vehr-sahye pah-lahs]
Vicomtesse Pierre du Fou	[vee-ko(n)-tehs pyehr dew foo]
Victor Borge	[veek-tohr bohrzh]
Victor Emmanuel	[veek-tohr ay-mah-newehl]
Victor Hugo	[veek-tohr ew-go]
Victor Hugo ® [Meilland]	[veek-tohr ew-go] [may(h) (y)a(n)]
Victor Hugo [Schwarz]	[veek-tohr ew-go]
Victor le Bihan	[veek-tohr luh bee-a(n)]
Victor Parmentier	[veek-tohr pahr-ma(n)-tyay]
Victor Verdier	[veek-tohr vehr-dyay]
Victor Velidan	[veek-tohr vuh-lee-da(n)]
Vidal Sassoon	[vee-dahl sah-so(n)]
Vierge de Cléry	[vyehr-zh duh klay-ree]
Vieux Château Certan ®	[vyuh shah-to sehr-ta(n)]
Vif Éclat	[veef ay-klah]
Ville d'Angers	[veel da(n)-zhay]
Ville d'Arcis sur Aube ®	[veel dahr-see sewr ob]
Ville d'Asnières	[veel dah-nyehr]
Ville d'Ettelbruck	[veel]
Ville de Bâle	[veel duh bahl]
Ville de Bar sur Seine ®	[veel duh bahr sewr sehn]
Ville de Bruxelles	[veel duh brew(k)-sehl]
Ville de Chine	[veel duh sheen]
Ville de Liffré ®	[veel duh lee-fray]
Ville de Londres	[veel duh lo(n)dr]
Ville de Paris	[veel duh pah-ree]
Ville de St Denis	[veel duh sah(n) duh-nee]
Ville de Toulouse	[veel duh too-looz]
Ville de Villeurbanne	[veel duh vee-luhr-bahn]
Ville de Ettelbruck	[veel duh]
Ville du Havre	[veel dew ahvr]
Ville du Perreux	[veel dew peh-hruh]
Ville du Roeulx	[veel dew hro-uhl]
Vinesse ®	[vee-nehs]
Violacée	[veeyo-lah-say]
Violaine	[veeyo-lehn]
Violette	[veeyo-leht]
Violette Parfum	[veeyo-leht pahr-fah(n)]
Violette Parfumée ®	[veeyo-leht pahr-few-may]
Violon d'Ingres ®	[veeyo-lo(n) dah(n)gr]

Virginale	[veer-zhee-nahl]
Vision Blanc	[vee-zeeyo(n) bla(n)]
Vision Blanc, Climbing	[vee-zyo(n) bla(n)]
Voeux de Bonheur	[vuh duh bo-nuhr]
Vogue	[vog]
Voie Lactée	[vwah lahk-tay]
Vol de Nuit	[vol duh nwee]
Voyager	[vwah-yah-zhay]
White Bon Silène	[bo(n) see-lehn]
White Cécile Brunner	[say-seel]
White Duchesse de Brabant	[dew-shehs duh brah-ba(n)]
White Fleurette ®	[fluh-reht]
White La France	[lah fra(n)s]
White Lafayette	[lah-fah-yet]
White Maman Cochet	[mah-ma(n) ko-sheh]
White Maman Cochet, Climbing	
	[mah-ma(n) ko-sheh]
White Meidiland ®	[meh-dee-la(n)]
White Noblesse ®	[no-blehs]
White Provence	[pro-va(n)s]
White Rose de Meaux	[hroz duh mo]
Xavier Olibo	[gzah-vyay o-lee-bo]
Yellow Cécile Brunner	[say-seel]
Yellow Cécile Brünner	[say-seel]
Yellow Cochet	[ko-sheh]
Yellow Maman Cochet	[mah-ma(n) ko-sheh]
Yolande d'Aragon	[eeyo-la(n)d dah-rah-go(n)]
Yves Piaget ®	[eev peeya-zheh]
Yvonne Rabier	[ee-von rah-byay]
Zéphirine Drouhin ®	[zay-fee-reen droo-ah(n)]
Zéphirine Drouhot	[zay-fee-reen droo-o]
Zoé	[zoay]

ROSIER HYBRIDE REMONTANT EUGÈNE FÜRST.

P. De Pannemaeker, pinx. et chromolith. Gand.

Eugène Fürst
[Technically not a German rose name]

A-L German

Aachener Dom	[AH-kh-en-er dohm]
Aaland	[AH-lahnd]
Aalsmeer Gold ®	[AHLS-mehr gold]
Abendglut ®	[AH-behnd-gloot]
Adam Messerich	[AH-dahm MEHS-eh-reeh(k)h]
Adolf Horstmann	[AH-dolf HORST-mahn]
Adolf's Red	[AH-dolfs]
Aennchen von Tharau	[AYN-h(k)hen fon tah-raow]
Agnes Bernauer ®	[AH-gnehs BEHR-nao-wer]
Agnes Kruse	[AH-gnehs KROO-zeh]
Agnes Winchel	[AH-gnehs VEHN-hkhel]
Albert Plapp	[AHL-behrt PLAHP]
Alden Biesen	[AHL-den BEE-sen]
Alfred Dietrich	[AHL-frehd DEET-rehc(k)h]
Alice Hoffmann	[AH-lehs HOFF-mahn]
Alma Bierbauer	[AHL-mah BEER-baow-er]
Alpenfee	[AHL-pen-fay]
Alt Marburg	[ahlt MAHR-boorg]
Alt Weinheim	[ahlt WIYN-hiym]
Amadeus ®	[ah-mah-DEH-oos]
Ambossfunken	[AM-bos-FOON-ken]
Ammonit	[ah-mo-NEHT]
Amulett ®	[ah-moo-LEHTT]
Andalusien	[ahn-dah-LOO-ziyen]
Andenken	[AHN-dehn-ken]
Anika ®	[AH-nee-kah]
Anna Scharsach]	[AHN-nah SHAHR-sahh(k)h]

Anna von Diesbach	[AHN-nah fon TEES-bahkh]
Anna Zinkeisen	[AHN-nah ZEHNK-iyzen]
Annabelle Kölle ®	[[AHN-nah-behl KUHL-leh]
Ännchen von Tharau	[AYN-c(k)hen fon tah-raow]
Anne of Geierstein	[GUY-er-shtiyn]
Annelies ®	[AH-neh-lees]
Anneliese Rothenberger	[ah-neh-LEE-seh RO-ten-ber-ger]
Anni Welter	[AH-nee VEHL-ter]
Antike 89 ®	[ahn-TEE-keh]
Antoine Schurz	[shoorts]
Apfelblüte ®	[AH-pfel-bl(e)oo-teh]
Arndt	[ahrnt]
Aschermittwoch	[AH-sher-MEHT-vohkh]
Asta von Parpart	[AHS-tah fon PAHR-part]
Astrid Späth	[AH-streed shpeht]
August Seebauer	[aow-GOOST ZAY-baow-er]
Augusta ®	[aow-GOO-stah]
Augusta Luise ®	[aow-GOO-stah loo-EE-zeh]
Aurelia Liffa	[aow-reh-lehah lehf-fah]
Baby Cécile Brunner	[BR(E)OO-ner]
Baby Tausendschön	[TAOW-zehnt-shuhn]
Bad Bergzabern ®	[bahd BEHRG-TSAH-behrn]
Bad Birnbach ®	[bahd BEERN-bahkh]
Bad Ems	[bahd EHMS]
Bad Füssing	[bahd f(e)oo-sing]
Bad Homburg	[bahd HOM-boorg]
Bad Nauheim ®	[bahd NAOW-hiym]
Bad Neuenahr	[bahd NOY-en-ahr]
Bad Wörishofen ®	[bahd WUH-rehs-ho-fen]
Baden-Baden	[bah-den BAH-den]
Barkarole	[bahr-kah-RO-leh]
Baron de Bonstetten	[BON-shteht-ten]
Bastei	[bahs-TIY]
Bayern Cover	[BIY-ern]
Bayerngold ®	[BIY-ern-gold]
Bayernland Cover ®	[BIY-ern-lahnd]
Bayerntraum ®	[BIY-ern-traowm]
Bayreuth	BIY-royt]
Bendigold	[BEHN-dee-gold]
Berlin	[behr-LEEN]

Berliner Luft ®   [behr-LEE-ner looft]
Bernard Däneke Rose
                      [BEHR-nard DAY-neh-keh ROH-zeh]
Bernd Clüver ®   [behrnt kl(e)oo-ver]
Bernstein Pol   [behrn-shtiyn pol]
Bernstein-Rose ®   [BEHRN-shtiyn RO-zeh]
Beyreuth   [biy-royt]
Bienenweide   [BEE-nehn-viy-deh]
Bischof Dr. Korum   [BEE-shof DOK-tor KO-room]
Bischofsstadt Paderborn ®
                      [BEESH-ofs-shtaht PAH-der-born]
Blaue Adria   [blaow-eh AH-dreh-ah]
Blenheim   [blehn-hiym]
Blühendes Barock ®   [BL(E)OO-hn-des bah-ROK]
Blühwunder ®   [BL(E)OO-VOON-der]
Blumenschmidt   [BLOO-men-shmit]
Blumenwunder   [BLOO-men-VOON-der]
Bona Weilschott   [BOH-nah VIYL-shot]
Bonn   [BON]
Brahm Datt   [brahm dat]
Brandenburg Gate   [BRAHN-den-boorg]
Brandenburg   [BRAHN-den-boorg]
Brautzauber ®   [BRAOWT-tsaow-ber]
Bremer Stadtmusikanten ®
                   [BREH-mer SHTAHT-moo-zee-KAHN-ten]
Brennende Liebe   [BREN-nen-deh LEE-beh]
Brennpunkt   [BREHN-poonkt]
Bubikopf ®   [BOO-bee-kopf]
Burg Baden   [boorg BAH-den]
Burghausen ®   [BOORG-haow-zen]
Burgund   [boor-GOOND]
Burkhard   [boork-hahrt]
Butzke's Snowflake   [BOOTS-kehs]
Cæcillie Scharsach   [shahr-sahkh]
Carl Luhn's Mystery Pink Noisette
                                   [kahrl loons]
Caroline Küster   [kah-ro-LEE-neh K(E)OO-ster]
Catherine von Würtemberg
          [kah-teh-REE-ne(h) fon [V(E)OOR-tehm-behrg]
Cécile Brunner   [BROON-er]

Conrad Ferdinand Meyer
               [KON-rahd FEHR-dee-nahnd MIY-er]
Dagmar Hastrup ®   [DAHG-mahr HAHS-troop]
Dagmar Späth   [DAHG-mahr shpeht]
Die Bloemhoffer   [dee bloom-ho-fer]
Die Rheinpfalz   [dee RIYN-pfahlts]
Die Schöne Tölzerin ® [dee SHUH-neh TUHL-tseh-rin]
Die Schönste   [dee SHUHN-steh]
Die Welt   [dee VEHLT]]
Dieter Wedel ®   [DEE-ter VEH-del]
Dietrich Woessner   [DEE-treh(k)h VUH-snehr
Direktor Rikala   [deh-REHK-tor reh-KAH-lah]
Doctor Faust   [DO-ktor faowst]
Domstadt Fulda   [DOM-shtat FOOL-dah]
Donauwalzer   [DO-naow-VAHL-tser]
Dornröschen   [DORN-ruhs-h(k)hen]
Dornröschenschloss Sababurg
               [DORN-ruhs-h(k)hen-shlos SAH-ba-boorg]
Dortmund ®]   [DORT-moond]
Dortmunder Kaiserhain ® [dort-MOON-der KIY-zer-hiyn]
Dr. Hermann Schulze-Delitzsch ®
             [DOK-tor HEHR-mahn shool-tseh-deh-leetsh]
Dr. Hurta   [DOK-tor HOOR-tah]
Dresden China   [DREHS-den CHEE-nah]
Dresden Doll Min   [DREHS-den]
Duchesse d'Auerstädt   [AOW-er-stayt]
Duett ®   [doo-eht]
Duftbella ®   [DOOFT-BEHL-lah]
Duftgold   [DOOFT-gold]
Duftrausch   [DOOFT-raowsh]
Dufts Berlin ®   [DOOFTS behr-LEEN]
Duftsparadies   [DOOFTSpah-rah-DEEZ]
Duftstar   [DOOFT]
Duftstern   [DOOFT-shtehrn]
Duftwolke   [DOOFT-vol-keh]
Duftzauber   [DOOFT-tsaow-ber]
Düsterlohe   [D(E)OO-ster-LO-heh]
Edelweiss   [EH-dehl-viys]
Eiberwein   [IY-ber-viyn]
Eiffelturm   [IY-fel-toorm]

Eisenach	[IY-zen-ah(k)h]
Elbfreude	[EHLB-FROY-deh]
Elfe	[EHL-feh]
Elfenreigen	[EHL-fen-RIY-gen]
Elisabeth Schnoltz	[eh-LEE-zah-beht SHNOLTS]
Elizabeth Fankhauser	
	[eh-LEE-zah-beht FAHNK-haow-zer]
Elsa Knoll	[EHL-zah knol]
Elsinore	[EHL-zee-NO-reh]
Emerickrose	[EH-meh-rehk-RO-zeh]
Emilie Verachter	[eh-MEE-lee-eh fehr-AHKH-ter]
Erfurt	[EHR-foort]
Erinnerung an Brod	[eh-REE-neh-roong ahn brod]
Erinnerung an Schloss Scharfenst	
	[eh-REE-neh-roong ahn shlos SHAHR-fenst]
Erlkönig	[EHRL-KUH-nig]
Ernst G. Dörell	[EHRNST geh duh-RELL]
Erotika ®	[eh-RO-tee-kah]
Esther	[EHS-ter]
Eugène Fürst	[f(e)oorst]
Eva Teschendorff	[EH-vah TEH-shen-torf]
Eva	[eh-vah]
Excellenz Kuntze	[ehx-seh-LEHNTS KOON-tseh]
Excellenz von Schubert	
	[ehx-seh-LEHNTS fon SHOO-behrt]
Fassadenzauber ®	[fah-SAH-den-TSAOW-ber]
Faust	[faowst]
Feldberg's Rosa Druschki	
	[FEHLD-behrgs RO-zah DROOSH-kee]
Felicia Teichmann	
	[feh-LEE-seh-ah TIYH(K)H-mahn]
Fellenberg	[FEHL-len-behrg]
Fern Kemp	[FEHRN Kehmp]
Fernand Tanne	[FEHR-nahnd TAHN-neh]
Fernande Krier	[fehr-NAHN-deh KREER]
Feuermeer	[FOY-er-mayr
Feuerwerk	[FOY-er-vehrk]
Feuerzauber	[FOY-er-tsaow-ber]
Ficksburg	[FEHKS-boorg]
Firlefanz	[FEHR-leh-fahnts]

Flammenmeer   [FLAHM-men-mayr]
Flammentanz   [FLAHM-men-tahnts]
Folklore   [fol-KLO-reh]
Forstmeister Heim   [FORST-MIY-ster HIYM]
Fragezeichen   [FRAH-geh-TSIY-h(k)hen]
Francisca Krüger

                               [frahn-TSEHS-kah KR(E)OO-ger]
Frankfurt am Main   [FRAHNK-foort ahm MIYN]
Frankfurt   [FRAHNK-foort]
Frans Hals   [frahns HAHLZ]
Frau Astrid Späth gestreift

                    [fraow AHS-trehd shpeht geh-shtriyft]
Frau Astrid Späth   [fraow AH-streed shpeht]
Frau Dagmar Hastrup

                    [fraow DAHG-mahr HAHS-troop]
Frau Dr. Hooftmann   [fraow DOK-tor HOFT-mahn]
Frau Dr. Schricker   [fraow DOK-tor SHREHK-ker]
Frau Eva Schubert   [fraow EH-vah SHOO-behrt]
Frau Hedwig Koschel   [fraow HEH-dvig Ko-shehl]
Frau Helen Verdiz   [fraow HEH-lehn fehr-DITS]
Frau Helene Videnz   [fraow heh-LEH-neh Fee-dehnts]
Frau Ida Münch   [fraow EE-dah M(E)OONH(K)H]
Frau Karl Druschki   [fraow kahrl DROOSH-kee]
Frau Lina Strassheim   [fraow LEE-nah SHTRAHS-hiym]
Frau Minka Rödiger   [fraow MEEN-kah RUH-deh-ger]
Frau O Plegg   [fraow O plehk]
Fräulein Ocatavia Hesse   [froy-liyn okTAH-vee-ah hehs-eh]
Frechdachs ®   [FREH(K)H-tahkhs]
Fredsrosen   [frehds-RO-zen}
Freifrau von Marschall   [FRIY-fraow fon MAHR-shahl]
Freiheitsglocke   [FRIY-hiyts-glok-keh]
Freiherr von Marschall   [FRIY-hehr fon MAHR-shahl]
Freisinger Morgenröte   [FRIY-sin-ger MOR-gen-RUH-teh]
Freude   [FROY-deh]
Friedrich Heyer   [freed-reh(k)h HIY-er]
Friesensöhne ®   [FREE-zen-ZUH-neh]
Friesia ®   [FREE-zeh-ah]
Fritz Nobis   [frehts NO-behs]
Fritz Walter   [frehts WAHL-ter]
Frohsinn ®   [FRO-zehn]

Fru Dagmar Hastrup   [DAHG-mahr HAHS-troop]
Früehlingszauber   [FR(E)OO-lings-tsaow-ber]
Frühlingsanfang   [FR(E)OO-lings-AHN-fahng]
Frühlingsduft   [FR(E)OO-lings-dooft]
Frühlingsgold ®   [FR(E)OO-lings-gold]
Frühlingsmorgen   [FR(E)OO-lings-mor-gen]
Frühlingsschnee   [FR(E)OO-lings-shnay]
Frühlingszauber   [FR(E)OO-lings-TSAOW-ber]
Fuggerstadt Augsburg ®   [FOOK-ker-staht AOWGS-boorg]
Funkuhr ®   [[FOONK-oor]
Fürstin von Pless   [F(E)OOR-stehn]
Futtaker Schlingrose   [FOOT-tah-ker shlehng-ro-zeh]
Gartenarchitekt Günther Schulze ®
  [GAHR-ten-AHR-h(k)heh-tehkt G(E)OON-ter SHOOL-tseh]
Gartenblut ®   [GAHR-ten-bloot]
Gartendirektor Lauche
                 [GAHR-ten-deh-REHK-tor LAOW-hkhe]
Gartendirektor Otto Linne
                 [GAHR-ten-deh-REHK-tor OT-to Lehn-neh]
Gartenfee   [GAHR-ten-fay]
Gartengold   [GAHR-ten-gold]
Gartenzauber   [GAHR-ten-tsaow-ber]
Gärtnerfreude ®   [GAYR-tner-FROY-deh]
Geheimrat Duisburg   [geh-HIYM-raht doo-EHS-boorg]
Gela Tepelmann   [GEH-lah TEH-pel-mahn]
Gelbe Dagmar Hastrup ®
                 [GEHL-beh DAHG-mahr HAAS-troop]
Gelbe Holstein   [GEHL-beh HOL-stiyn]
Gelber Kobold ®   [GEHL-beh KO-bolt]
Germanica   [gehr-MAH-neh-kah]
Geschwind's Gorgeous   [geh-SHVEHN(D)S]
Geschwind's Nordlandrose
                 [geh-SHVEHN(D)S nord-lahnd ro-zeh]
Geschwind's Orden   [geh-SHVEHN(D)S OR-den]
Geschwind's Schönste   [geh-SHVEHN(D)S SHUHN-steh]
Giesebrecht   [GEE-zeh-breh(k)ht]
Giessenrose   [Gee-sen-ro-zeh]
Gisselfeld ®   [GEHS-sel-fehld]
Gitta Grummer   [GEE-tah GROOM-mer]
Gitte   [GEHT-teh]

Gletscherfee ®	[GLEH-tsher-fay]
Glücksburg	[GL(E)OOKS-boorg]
Goethe	[GUH-teh]
Gold Rausch	[GOLD raowsh]
Goldbusch	[GOLD-boosh]
Golddorf Seppenrade	[GOLD-dorf SEHP-pen-rah-deh]
Golden Holstein	[gol-den HOL-shtiyn]
Goldener Olymp	[GOL-deh-ner o-L(E)OOMP] ?
Goldener Sommer	[GOL-deh-ner SOM-mer]
Goldfächer	[GOLD-FEH-h(k)her]
Goldfassade	[GOLD-fah-SAH-deh]
Goldkrone	[GOLD-KRO-neh]
Goldmarie	[GOLD-mah-REE]
Goldrausch	[GOLD-raowsh]
Goldregen	[GOLD-REH-gen]
Goldschatz ®	[GOLD-shats]
Goldstein ®	[GOLD-shtiyn]
Goldstern ®	[GOLD-shtehrn]
Goldtopas ®	[GOLD-TO-pahz]
Gottfried Keller	[GOT-freed KEHL-ler]
Graf Fritz von Hochberg	[graaf frehts fon HOHKH-behrg]
Graf Lennart	[graaf LEHN-nahrt]
Gräfin Esterhazy	[GRAY-fin ehs-ter-HAH-zee]
Gräfin Marie-Henriette Chotek	
[GRAY-fin mah-REE-hen-ree-EHT-te HKHO-tehk]	
Gräfin Sonja ®	[GRAY-fin SON-iya]
Grande Walzer ®	[vahl-tser]
Grossherzog Friedrich von Baden	
[GROS-HEHR-tsog FREE-drih(k)h fon BAH-den]	
Grossmütterchen	[GROS-m(e)oo-ter-h(k)hen]
Gruss an Aachen	[groos ahn AH-hkhen]
Gruss an Angeln ®	[groos ahn AHN-geln]
Gruss an Baden-Baden	[groos ahn BAH-den-BAH-den]
Gruss an Bayern ®	[groos ahn BIY-ern]
Gruss an Berlin	[groos ahn behr-LEEN]
Gruss an Breinnegg	[groos ahn BRIY-nehk]
Gruss an Coburg	[groos ahn KO-boorg]
Gruss an Freundorf	[groos ahn FROYN-dorf]
Gruss an Friedberg	[groos ahn freed-behrg]
Gruss an Germershausen	[groos ahn GEHR-mers-haow-zen]

Gruss an Heidelberg	[groos ahn HIY-del-behrg]
Gruss an Koblenz	[groos ahn KO-blehnts]
Gruss an Oldenburg	[groos ahn OL-den-boorg]
Gruss an Stuttgart ®	[groos ahn SHTOOT-gahrt]
Gruss an Teplitz	[groos ahn TEHP-lehts]
Gruss an Zabern	[groos ahn TSAH-bern]
Gudhemsrosen	[[good-hehms-RO-zen]
Gustav Frahm	[GOO-stahf frahm]
Gustav Grünerwald	[GOO-stahf GR(E)OO-ner-wahld]
Gütersloh	[G(E)OO-ters-loh]
Hackeburg	[HAH-keh-boorg]
Hagenbecks Tierpark ®	[HAH-gen-behks TEER-pahrk]
Hamburg	[HAHM-boorg]
Hamburger Deern ®	[HAHM-boor-ger dehrn]
Händel ®	[HAYN-del]
Hanne	[HAHN-eh]
Hannover's Weisse ®	[HAH-no-fers VIY-seh]
Hans Christian Andersen	[hahns KREE-stian AHN-der-sen]
Hans Erni	[hahns EHR-nee]
Hans Mackart	[hahns MAHK-kahrt]
Hans Rosenthal	[hahns RO-zen-tahl]
Hansa	[HAHN-zah]
Hansaland ®	[HAHN-zah-lahnd]
Hansa-Park ®	[HAHN-zah-pahrk]
Hansestadt Lübeck	[HAHN-ze-shtaht L(E)OO-behk]
Harlekin ®	[HAHR-leh-kin]
Harmonie	[hahr-mo-NEE]
Harry Oppenheimer	[HAH-ree OH-pen-hiy-mer]
Heckenzauber	[HEHK-ken-tsaow-ber]
Hede Grimm	[HEH-deh grehm]
Heidefeuer ®	[HIY-deh-foy-er]
Heidekind ®	[HIY-deh-kehnd]
Heidekönigin ®	[HIY-deh-KUH-nee-gehn]
Heidelberg	[HIY-dehl-berg]
Heidelinde ®	[HIY-deh-LEEN-deh]
Heidepark ®	[HIY-deh-pahrk]
Heideröslein Nozomi ®	
	[HIY-deh-RUHZ-liyn no-TSO-mee]
Heideröslein	[HIY-deh-RUHZ-liyn]
Heideschnee ®	[HIY-deh-shnay]

Heidesommer ®	[HIY-deh-SOM-er]
Heidetraum	[HIY-deh-traowm]
Heidi ®	[HIY-dee]
Heike	[HIY-keh]
Hein Mück ®	[hiyn m(e)ook]
Heinfels ®	[hiyn-fehls]
Heinrich Blanc ®	[hiyn-reh(k)h]
Heinrich Conrad Söth	[HIYN-reh(k)h KON-rahd SUHT]
Heinrich Karsch	[HIYN-reh(k)h KAHRSH]
Heinrich Keller	[HIYN-reh(k)h KEHL-ler]
Heinrich Münch	[HIYN-reh(k)h M(e)oonh(k)h]
Heinrich Schultheis	[HIYN-reh(k)h SHOOLT-hiys]
Heinrich Wendland	[HIYN-reh(k)h VEHND-lahnd]
Heinz Erhardt ®	[HIYNTS EHR-hahrt]
Heinz Treffinger ®	[HIYNTS TREHF-fin-ger]
Heinzelmännchen ®	[HIYN-tsel-MEHN-h(k)hen]
Heimatmelodie ®	[HIY-maht-meh-loh-DEE]
Helen Keller ®	[HEH-lehn KEHL-ler]
Helen Traubel	[HEH-lehn TRAOW-bel]
Helene Schoen	[heh-LEH-neh SHUHN]
Helga ®	[HEHL-gah]
Helmut Kohl	[HEHL-moot kohl]
Helmut Schmidt ®	[HEL-moot shmeht]
Herbstfeuer	[HEHRBST-foy-er]
Herman Steyn	[HEHR-mahn shtiyn]
Hermann Lindecke	[HEHR-mahn LEHN-deh-keh]
Hermann Löns	[HEHR-mahn luhns]
Hermann Schmidt	[Hehr-mahn shmeht]
Herz As	[hehrts ahs]
Herzblättchen Pol	[HEHRTS-BLAYT-h(k)hen pol]
Herz-Dame	[HEHRTS-DA-meh]
Herzensgruss	[HEHRT-tsens-groos]
Herzog von Windsor ®	[HEHR-tsog fon VIN-tsor]
Herzogin Viktoria Adelheid von Coburg-Gotha	
	[HEHR-tso-gehn vehk-TOH-reh-ah AHDEL-hiyd fon
	KOH-boorg-GOH-tah]
Hetzel	[HEH-tsel]
Hilda Heinemann	[HEHL-dah HIY-neh-mahn]
Hilde	[HEHL-deh]
Hilde Apelt	[HEHL-deh AH-pehlt]

Hilde Steinert	[HEHL-deh SHTIY-nert]
Hildenbrandseck	[HEHL-den-brahnd-sehk]
Himmelsauge	[HEHM-mels-AOW-geh]
Himmelsstürmer	[HEHM-mels-sht(e)oor-mer]
Hinrich Gaede	[HEHN-reh(k)h GAY-deh]
Hiroschimasche Kindern	
	[hee-RO-shee-MAH-sheh KEHN-dern]
Hoffmann von Fallersleben	
	[HOF-mahn fon FAHL-lers-leh-ben]
Hofgärtner Kalb	[hof-GAYR-tner kahlb]
Holländerin	[HO-layn-deh-rehn]
Holstein	[HOL-stiyn]
Holsteinperle	[HOL-stiyn-pehr-leh]
Holstentor ®	[HOLS-ten-tohr]
Holtermann's Gold	[HOL-ter-mahns gold]
Honigmond	[HOH-nehg-mohnd]
Horstmann's Rosenresli	
	[HORST-mahns RO-zen-REH-zlee]
Horstmanns Leuchtfeuer	
	[HORST-mahns LOYH(K)HT-foy-er]
Hurdalsrose	[HOOR-dahls-ro-zeh]
Ida Elizabeth	[EE-dah eh-LEE-zah-beht]
Ilmenau ®	[EHL-men-aow]
Ilse Haberland	[EHL-zeh HAH-ber-land]
Ilse Krohn Superior	[EHL-zeh Krohn]
Immensee	[EHM-en-zeh]
Ina Bender	[EE-nah behn-der]
Ingrid Bergman ®	[EHN-greed BEHRG-mahn]
Ingrid Weibull ®	[EHN-greed VIY-bool]
Insel Mainau ®	[EHN-zel MIY-naow]
Inspektor Blohm	[ehns-PEHK-tor blohm]
Irene von Dänemark	[EE-reh-neh fon DEH-neh-mahrk]
J.F. Müller	[yot. f. M(e)oo-ler]
Janine Herholdt	[HEHR-holt]
Jean Rosenkrantz	[RO-zen-krahnts]
Johann Strauss	[YO-hahn shtraows]
Johanna Röpcke	[yo-HAHN-nah RUHP-keh]
Johannes Becker	[yo-HAH-nehs BEH-ker]
Johannes Boettner	[yo-HAH-nehs BUHT-ner]
Johannes Rau	[yo-HAH-nehs raow]

Johannes Schultheis ®   [yo-HAH-nehs SHOOLT-hiys]
Johannisfeuer ®   [yo-HAH-nehs-foy-er]
Johannisröschen   [yo-HAH-nehs-RUHZ-h(k)hen]
Josef Rothmund   [YO-zehf ROT-moond]
Juleschke   [yoo-LEH-shkeh]
Justizrat Dr Hessert
              [yoo-STEETS-raht DOK-tor HEHS-sehrt]
Kaiserin Auguste Viktoria
           [KIY-zeh-rin aow-GOO-steh vehk-TOH-reh-ah]
Kaiserin Farah   [KIY-zeh-rin
Kaiserin Friedrich   [KIY-zeh-rin FREED-reh(k)h
Kardinal   [kahr-dee-NAHL]
Karl Diehl   [kahrl deel]
Karl Fischer ®   [kahrl feh-sher]
Karl Förster   [kahrl FUHR-ster]
Karl Heinz Hanisch ®   [kahrl hiynts HAH-nish]
Karl Herbst   [kahrl hehrbst]
Karl Höchst ®   [kahrl huhkst]
Karl Weinhausen   [kahrl VIYN-haow-zen]
Karlsruhe   [kahrls-ROO-heh]
Kassel   [KAHS-sel]
Katharina Zeimet   [kah-tah-ree-nah TSIY-meht]
Käthe Duvigneau   [kay-teh]
Kersbergen Pol   [KEHRS-behr-gen pol]
Kessi ®   [KEHS-see]
Kiese   [KEE-zeh]
Kirsten   [KEHR-sten]
Kirsten Klein   [KEHR-sten kliyn]
Kirsten Poulsen   [KEHR-sten POOL-sen]
Klaus Groth   [klaows grot]
Klaus Störtebeker   [klaows SHTUHR-teh-beh-ker]
Kleine Dortmund ®   [KLIY-neh DORT-moond]
Kleine Dortmunderin   [KLIY-neh DORT-moon-deh-rehn]
Kleine Eva ®   [KLIY-neh EH-vah]
Kleine Regina ®   [KLIY-neh reh-GEE-nah]
Kleopatra ®   [kleho-PAH-trah]
Knirps ®   [kneerps]
Köln am Rhein   [kuhln ahm riyn]
Kölner Karneval   [KUHL-ner KAHR-neh-vahl]]
Kommerzienrat   [ko-MEHR-tsyen-raht]

Kommodore	[ko-mo-DO-reh]
Konfetti	[kon-FEHT-tee]
König Ludwig-Rose	[KUH-nig LOOD-veeg RO-zeh]
Königin Beatrix	[KUH-neh-gehn beh-ah-trehx]
Königin der Rosen	[KUH-neh-gehn dehr RO-zen]
Königin Juliana	[KUH-neh-gehn yoo-leh-AH-nah]
Königin Margrethe	[KUH-neh-gehn mahr-GREH-teh]
Königin von Dänemark	
	[KUH-neh-gehn fon DAY-neh-mahrk]
Königin Wilhelmina ®	
	[KUH-neh-gehn vehl-hehl-MEE-nah]
Königliche Hoheit	[KUH-nehg-leh-h(k)heh HO-hiyt]
Konrad Adenauer Rose	
	[KON-rahd AH-deh-naower RO-ze]
Konrad Henkel ®	[KON-rahd Hehn-kehl]
Kontiki	[kon-TEH-kee]
Kontrast ®	[KON-trahst]
Koralle	[ko-RAHL-leh]
Krause Macrantha	[KRAOW-zeh]
Kristall ®	[kreh-STAHLL]
Kristin	[KREHS-tehn]
Krönborg ®	[KRUHN-borg]
Kronjuwel ®	[KROHN-yoo-vehl]
Kronprinzessin Victoria ®	
	[KROHN-prehn-TSEHS-sin vehk-TOH-reh-ah]
Kronprinzessin Viktoria von Preussen	
	[KROHN-prehn-TSEHS-ehn vehk-TOH-reh-ah fon PROY-en]
Küpferkönigin ®	[K(E)OO-pfer-KUH-neh-gehn]
Lagerfeld	[LAH-ger-fehld]
Lagerfeuer ®	[LAH-ger-FOY-er]
Lavaglut ®	[LAH-vah-gloot]
Legacy of Eva Zeiner	[EH-vah TSIY-ner]
Legacy of George Wunschel	[voon-shel]
Legacy of Ludwig Barth	[lood-vehg bahrt]
Legacy of the Schmeder Family	[shmeh-der]
Lenzburger Duft	[LEHNTS-boor-ger dooft]
Leuchtstern	[LOYH(K)HT-shtehrn]
Leverkusen	[LEH-ver-KOO-zen]
Lichtblick	[LEH(K)HT-blehk]

Lichtkönigin Lucia ®
    [LEH(K)HT-kuh-neh-gehn loo-SEE -ah]
Lichtloh ®   [LEH(K)HT-loh]
Liebeslied ®   [LEE-behs-leed]
Liebestraum   [LEE-behs-traowm]
Liebeszauber ®   [LEE-behs-tsaow-ber]
Linderof   [LEHN-der-ohf]
Lissy Horstmann   [HORST-mahn]
Lotte Günthart   [LO-teh G(E)OONT-hahrt]
Lübeck   [L(E)OO-behk]
Lübecker Rotspon ®   [L(E)OO-beh-ker ROT-shpohn]
Lucinde ®   [loo-SEHN-deh]
Ludwigshafen am Rheim ®   [LOOD-vehgs-hah-fen ahm riyn]
Lustige   [LOO-steh-geh]

ROSE NOTES:

ROSE HYBRIDE REMONTANTE "LOUIS VAN HOUTTE"

Louis Van Houtte
[Technically not a German rose name]

M-Z GERMAN

Madeleine Seltzer	[mah-dlayn SEHL-tser]
Magaliesburg Roos	[mah-gah-LEES rohs]
Maigold	[MIY-gold]
Mainauduft ®	[MIY-naow-dooft]
Mainaufeuer ®	[MIY-naow-FOY-er]
Mainauperle ®	[MIY-naow-PEHR-leh]
Mainzer Fastnacht ®	[MIYN-tser FAHS-(t)nahkht)
Mainzer Wappen	[MIYN-tser vah-pen]
Maiwunder	[MIY-voon-der]
Maja Mauser	[MAHY-ah MAOW-zer]
Maja Oetker ®	[MAHY-ah UHT-ker]
Majolika ®	[mah-YOH-leh-kah]
Mannheim	[MAHN-hiym]
Märchenkönigin ®	[MEHR-h(k)hen-KUH -neh-gehn]
Märchenland	[MEHR-h(k)hen-lahnd]
Margaret Wasserfall	[MAHR-gah-reht VAHS-ser-fahl]
Margaretha Adelheid	[mahr-gah-REH-tah AH-del-hiyd]
Maria Graebner	[mah-REE-ah GRAYB-ner]
Maria Hofker ®	[mah-REE-ah HOF-ker]
Maria Mathilda	[mah-REE-ah mah-TEHL-dah]
Maria Stern	[mah-REE-ah shtehrn]
Marie Dermar	[mah-REE dehr-MAHR]
Marietta Gräfin Silva Tarouca	
[mah-ree-EHT-ta GRAY-fin SEHL-vah tah-ROO-kah]	
Marlena ®	[mahr-LEH-nah]
Marselisborg ®	[mahr-seh-lehs-borg]
Martha	[mahr-tah]

Maskotte	[mahs-KOT -teh]
Matador	[mah-tah-DOR]
Matterhorn	[MAHT-ter-horn]
Max Graf	[mahx grahf]
Mechtilde von Neuerburg	
	[mehkh-TEHL -deh fon NOY-er-boorg]
Mein München	[miyn M(E)OON-h(k)hen]
Mein Schöner Garten ®	[miyn SHUH-ner GAHR-ten]
Meine Oma	[miy-neh OH-mah]
Mevrouw Amélie Müller	[M(E)OO-ler]
Minna Kordes	[MEHN-nah KOR-dehs]
Mlle Cécile Brunner	[BR(E)OO-ner]
Mlle Franziska Krüger	[frahn-TSEHS-kah KR(E)OO-ger]
Mme Cécile Brunner	[BR(E)OO-ner]
Mme Joseph Schwartz	[shwahrts]
Mme Knorr	[knorr]
Mme la Duchesse d'Auerstädt	[DAOW-er-steht]
Mme Zöetmans	[TSUHT-mahns]
Mme. Herman Haefliger	[HEHR-man HEHF-leh-ger]
Mme. Neumann	[NOY-mahn]
Morgengruss	[MOR-gen-groos]
Morgenrot ®	[MOR-gen-roht]
Morgenröte	[MOR-gen-ruh-teh]
Morgenstern ®	[MOR-gen-shtehrn]
Mossman	[MOSS-mahn]
Mozart	[MOH-tsahrt]
Mühle Hermsdorf	[M(E)OO-leh HEHRMS-dorf]
München Kindl	[M(E)OON-h(k)hen Kehn-del]
München	[M(E)OON-h(k)hen]
Münchener Fasching	[M(E)OON-h(k)hen-er fah-shing]
Münchner Herz ®	[M(E)OON-h(k)hner hayrts]
Münchner Kindl ®	[M(E)OONH(K)H-ner kehndl]
Münster	[M(E)OON-ster]
Münsterland ®	[M(E)OON-ster-lahnd]
Musikantenland ®	[moo-zee-KAHN-ten-lahnd]
Muttertag	[MOO-ter-tahg]
Myra Stegmann	[MEE-rah SHTEHG-mahn]
Naheglut ®	[NAH-heh-gloot]
Narzisse	[nahr-TSEHS-seh]
Natascha	[nah-TAH-shah]

Nelkenrose	[NEHL-ken-RO-ze]
Neue Revue ®	[noy-eh reh-v(e)oo]
Nina Weibull ®	[NEE-nah WIY-bool]
Nordhausen	[nord-HAOW-zen]
Nymphe Tepla	[N(E)OOM-fe TEHP-lah]
Nymphenburg	[N(E)OOM-fen-boorg] ?
Oberbürgermeister Boock Pol	
	[OH-ber-B(E)OOR-ger-miy-ster bok pol]
Obergärtner Wiebicke	[O-ber-gayr-tner VEE-beh-keh]
Ocatvius Weld	[ok-TAH-vioos vehld]
OEkonomierat Echtermeyer	
	[uh-koh-noh-MEE-raht EH(K)H-tehr-miy-er]
Ohl	[ol]
Opa Pötschke	[O-pah PUH-tshkeh]
Opal Brunner	[O-pahl BROON-ner]
Orange Muttertag	[MOOT-ter-tahg]
Oskar Cordel	[OS-kahr KOR-del]
Oskar Scheerer	[OS-kahr SHEH-rer]
Palmengarten Frankfurt ®	
	[PAHL-men-gahr-ten FRAHNK-foort]
Parkdirektor Riggers ®	
	[PAHRK-dee-REHK-tor REHG-gers]
Parkfeuer	[PAHRK-foy-er]
Parkzauber	[PAHRK-tsaow-ber]
Parkzierde	[PAHRK-tseer-deh]
Patricia Beucher	[pah-TREE-tsiah BOY-h(k)her]
Patricia Oppmann	[pah-TREE-tsiah OP-mahn]
Perle von Britz	[PEHR-leh fon BREHTS]
Perle von Heidelberg	[PEHR-leh fon HIY-del-behrg]
Perle von Weissenstein	[PEHR-leh fon WIY-sen-shtiyn]
Peter Frankenfeld ®	[PEH-ter FRAHN-ken-fehld]
Peter Wessel	[PEH-ter VEHS-el]
Pfälzer Gold ®	[PFEHL-tser gold]
Pharisäer	[fah-ree-say-er]
Pink Frau Karl Druschki	[fraow kahrl DROOSH-kee]
Pink Gruss an Aachen	[groos ahn AH-hkhen]
Pink Kardinal	[kahr-dee-NAHL]
Pink Traumland ®	[TRAOWM-lahnd]
Polareis ®	[po-LAHR-iys]
Polarsonne ®	[po-LAHR-ZON-neh]

Polarstern ®   [po-LAHR-shtehrn]
Poulsen's Gruppenrose
                                      [POOL-sen's GROO-pehn-RO-zeh]
Primerose Sistau Pol   [SEHS-taow]
Prince Charles d'Aremberg   [AH-rehm-behrg]
Princesse Christine von Salm   [krehs-tee-neh fon zahlm]
Prinz Eugen von Savoyen
                                      [prehnts OY-gehn fon sah-VOY-en]
Prinz Hamlet   [prehnts HAHM-leht]
Prinz Hirzeprinzchen
                          [prehnts HEER-tseh-PREHN-tsh(k)hen]
Prinzessin Irrlieb   [prehn-TSEHS-sin EHRR-leeb]
Prinzessin M. von Arenberg
                          [prehn-TSEHS-sin M. fon AH-ren-behrg]
Purpurtraum 2000 ®   [POOR-poor]
Rainer Maria Rilke   [RIY-ner mah-REE-ah REHL-keh]
Raubritter   [raowb-reh-ter]
Ravensberg   [RAH-vens-behrg]
Red Berlin   [behr-leen]
Red Dagmar   [DAHG-mahr]
Red Frau Dagmar Hastrup
                                      [fraow DAHG-mahr HAHS-troop]
Red Heidetraum   [HIY-deh-traowm]
Red Max Graf   [mahx grahf]
Regensberg   [REH-gens-behrg]
Regierungsrath Rottenburger'
                          [reh-GEE-roongs-raht ROT-ten-boor-ger]
Reichspräsident von Hindenburg
                [RIYH(K)HS-preh-zee-dehnt fon HEHN-den-boorg]
Reine Olga de Würtemberg   [V(E)OOR-tehm-behrg]
Reinhard Bädecker   [RIYN-hahrd BAY-deh-ker]
Rekordblüher   [reh-KORD-bl(e)oo-her]
Rheinaupark ®   [RIY-naow-pahrk]
Ruhm von Steinfurth   [room fon SHTIYN-foort]
Richard Strauss   [REH-h(k)hahrd shtraows]
Richard Trauber   [REH-h(k)hahrd TRAOW-ber]
Rina Herholdt   [REE-nah hehr-holt]
Ritter von Barmstede
                                      [REHT-ter fon BAHRM-shteh-deh]
Rittertum   [REHT-ter-toom]

Ritz   [rehts]
Rödhätte ?   [RUHD-hay-teh]
Rödinghausen ®   [RUH-ding-haow-zen]
Roman Herzog ®   [ro-MAHN HEHRT-tsog]
Romanze ®   [ro-MAHN-tseh]
Rosa Zwerg   [ROH-zah tsvehrg]
Rosamunde   [ro-zah-MOON-deh]
Rosarium Glücksburg ®
                    [ro-ZAH-rehoom GL(E)OOKS-boorg]
Rosarium Uetersen ®   [ro-ZAH-rehoom (E)OO-ter-sehn]
Rose de Rescht   [rehsht]
Rose Hindukusch   [RO-zeh HEHN-doo-koosh]
Rose Neumann   [RO-zeh NOY-mahn]
Rose von Berga ®   [ROH-zeh fon BEHR-gah]
Rosenau   [ROH-zeh-naow]
Rosendorf Schmitshausen
                    [ROH-zen-dorf SHMEHTS-haow-zen]
Rosendorf Sparrieshoop ®
                    [ROH-zen-dorf SHPAHR-rees-hohp]
Rosendorf Steinfurth   [ROH-zen-dorf SHTIYN-foort]
Rosendorf Ufhoven   [ROH-zen-dorf oof-HO-ven]
Rosendorf   [ROH-zen-dorf]
Rosenelfe   [ROH-zen-EHL-feh]
Rosenfee ®   [ROH-zen-fay]
Rosenfest   [ROH-zen-fest]
Rosenholm   [ROH-zen-holm]
Rosenmärchen   [ROH-zen-MAYR-h(k)hen
Rosenprinzessin   [ROH-zen-prehn-TSEHS-sin]
Rosenprinzessin Andrea ®
                    [ROH-zen-prehn-TSEHS-sin ahn-DREH-ah]
Rosenprofessor Sieber ®
                    [ROH-zen-pro-FEHS-sor ZEE-ber]
Rosenreigen ®   [ROH-zen-riy-gen]
Rosenresli   [ROH-zen-rehz-lee]
Rosenrot ®   [ROH-zen-rot]
Rosenstadt Zweibrücken ®
                    [ROH-zen-shtaht tsviy-BR(E)OO-ken]
Rosentanz   [ROH-zen-tahnts]
Rosenthal   [ROH-zen-tahl]
Rosenwalzer ®   [ROH-zen-vahl-tser]

Rosenwunder	[ROH-zen-VOON-der]
Rosenzauber ®	[ROH-zen-tsaow-ber]
Rote Hannover	[ROH-teh hah-NO-ver]
Rote Krimrose	[ROH-teh KREEM-roh-zeh]
Rote Max Graf ®	[ROH-teh mahx grahf]
Rote Mozart ®	[ROH-teh MO-tsahrt]
Rote Woge ®	[ROH-teh VOH-geh]
Rotelfe ®	[ROHT-EHL-feh]
Roter Champagner	[ROH-ter shahm-PAH-n(e)er]
Roter Kobold ®	[ROH-ter KOH-bolt]
Roter Stern	[ROH-ter shtehrn]
Rotes Meer	[ROH-tes Mayr]
Rotesmeer	[ROH-tes-mayr]
Rottkäppchen	[rot-KAYP-hk)hen
Rudelsburg	[ROO-dels-boorg]
Rudolf Alexander Schröder	[ROO-dolf AH-leh-xahn-der]
Rudolf von Bennigsen	[ROO-dolf fon BEHN-nehg-sen]
Ruhm von Steinfurth	[room fon SHTIYN-foort]
Ruth Leuwerik	[root loy-veh-rehk]
Saarlandwelle ®	[SAHR-lahnd-VEHL-leh
Sachsengruss	[SAH-hkhsen-groos]
Salzajubiläum	[yoo-beh-LAY-oom]
Salzburg	[SAHLTS-boorg]
Sangerhausen	[SAN-ger-haow-zen]
Sankt Florian	[sahnkt FLO-reh-ahn]
Scharlachglut	[SHAHR-lahkh-gloot]
Schwarzer Samt	[SHWAHR-tser SAHMT
Schwarzwaldfeuer ®	[SHWAHRTS-vahld-foy-er]
Schwarzwaldmädel ®	[SHWAHRTS-wahld-MAY-del]
Schweizer Garten ®	[SHWIY-tser GAHR-ten]
Schleswig 87 ®	[SHLEHS-vehg]
Schloss Balthasar ®	[shlos BAHL-tah-zahr]
Schloss Friedenstein	shlos FREE-den-shtiyn]
Schloss Glücksburg ®	[shlos GL(E)OOKS-boorg]
Schloss Heidegg ®	[shlos hiy-DEK]
Schloss Mannheim ®	[shlos MAHN-hiym]
Schloss Seusslitz	[shlos SOYS-lehts]
Schlossgarten	[SHLOS-gahr-ten]
Schmetterling	[SHMEHT-ter-ling]
Schneeberg	[SHNAY-behrg]

Schnee-Eule ®	[SHNAY-oy-leh]
Schneeflocke ®	[SHNAY-flo-keh]
Schneekönigin	[SHNAY-kuh-neh-gehn]
Schneekoppe	[SHNAY-ko-peh]
Schneeküsschen	[SHNAY-k(e)oos-h(k)hen]
Schneelicht	[SHNAY-leh(k)ht]
Schneeschirm	[SHNAY-shehrm]
Schneesturm ®	[SHNAY-shtoorm]
Schneewaltzer ®	[SHNAY-val-tser]
Schneeweisschen ®	[SHNAY-viys-h(k)hen
Schneewittchen ®	[SHNAY-veht-h(k)hen]
Schneezwerg	[SHNAY-tsvehrg]
Schoener's Nutkana	[SHUH-ners noot-kah-nah]
Scholle's Golden Moss	[SHOL-lehs]
Schöne Berlinerin ®	[SHUH-neh behr-LEE-neh-rin]
Schöne Dortmunderin ®	[SHUH-neh dort-MOON-deh-rin]
Schöne Münchnerin	
	[SHUH-neh M(E)OON-h(k)heh-rin]
Schöne von Holstein Pol	[SHUH-neh fon HOL-shtiyn pol]
Schöne von Holstein	[SHUH-neh fon hol-shtiyn]
Schuss ®	[shooss]
Schwabenmädel	[SHVAH-ben-may-del]
Schwanensee ®	[SHVAH-nen-zay]
Schwarze Madonna ®	[SHVAHR-tseh mah-DON-nah]
Schweizer Gold	[SHVIY-tser gold]
Schweizer Gruss ®	[SHVIY-tser groos]
Schweizer Woche ®	[SHVIY-tser VO-hkheh]
Schwerin	[SHWEH-rin]
Sebastian Kneipp	[seh-BAH-steh-ahn kniyp]
Sebastian Schultheis	[seh-BAH-steh-ahn shoolt-hiys]
Silberlachs	[SEHL-ber-lahkhs]
Silken Laumann ®	[LAOW-man]
Sommerabend ®	[SOM-mer-ah-bend]
Sommerduft ®	[SOM-mer-dooft]
Sommerfreude ®	[SOM-mer-froy-deh]
Sommermärchen ®	[SOM-mer-mayr-h(k)hen]
Sommermelodie ®	[SOM-mer-meh-loh-DEE]
Sommermond ®	[SOM-mer-mond]
Sommermorgen ®	[SOM-mer-MOR-gen]
Sommerschnee ®	[SOM-mer-shnay]

Sommertag	[SOM-mer-tahg]
Sommerwind ®	[SOM-mer-wind]
Sondermeldung	[SON-der-MEHLL-doong]
Sonja Horstmann	[SON-yah HORST-mahn]
Sonnenkind ®	[SON-nen-kehnd]
Sonnenschirm ®	[SON-nen-sheerm]
Späth's Jubiläum	[shpayts yoo-bee-LAY-oom]
Spielplatz	[shpeel-plahts]
Sport of Rodhätte	[ROD-hayt-teh]
Stadt Basel ®	[shtaht BAH-zel]
Stadt den Helder	[shtaht den HEHL-der]
Stadt Eltville	[shtaht EHLT-veel]
Stadt Hildescheim ®	[shtaht HEHL-deh-shiym]
Stadt Hockenheim	[shtaht HOK-ken-hiym]
Stadt Kiel ®	[shtaht keel]
Stadt Rosenheim	[shtaht ROH-zen-hiym]
Stadt Würzburg	[shtaht vuurts-boorg]
Stadtrat Meyn	[STAHT-raht MIYN]
Stämmler	[SHTAYM-ler]
Steffi Graf	[SHTEHF-fee graaf]
Stellmacher	[SHTEHL-mah-hkher]
Sterkmanns	[SHTEHRK-mahns]
Sternenflor ®	[SHTEHR-nen-flor]
Stilfontein Rose	[SHTEHL-fon-tiyn ROH-zeh]
Strombergzauber ®	[SHTROM-behrg-TSAOW-ber]
Sympathie	[s(e)oom-pah-TEE]
Symphonie	[s(e)oom-fo-NEE]
Taunusblümchen	[TAOW-noos-bl(e)oom-h(k)hen]
Tausendschön	[TAOW-zehnd-shuhn]
Theodor Körner ®	[TEH-oh-dor KUHR-ner]
Thérèse Bauer	[baow-er]
Till Uhlenspiegel	[tehl OO-len-shpee-gel]
Toorenburg	[TOH-ren-boorg]
Träumerei ®	[troy-meh-RIY]
Traumland	[TRAOWM-land]
Travemünde ®	[trah-veh-M(E)OON-deh]
Trollhättan	[TROL-hay-tahn]
Trompeter von Säckingen	[trom-PEH-ter fon SAYK-king-en]
Tynwald	[tehn-wahld]
Ulla Land	[OOL-lah lahnd]

Ulmer Münster ®	[OOL-mer M(E)OON-ster]
Ulrich Brunner	[OOL-rih(k)h BROO-ner]
Unermüdliche	[OON-er-M(E)OO-dleh-h(k)heh]
Uwe Seeler	[OO-veh Zay-ler]
Valentin Ruch	[VAH-lehn-teen roohkh]
Vatertag ®	[FAH-ter-tahg]
Veilchenblau	[FIYL-h(k)hen-blaow]
Verbesserte Tantaus Triumph	
	[fehr-BEHS-sehr-teh TAHN-taows treh-OOMF]
Veronika	[feh-RO-nee-kah]
Verschurren	[vehr-SHOO-ren]
Vierlanden	[feer-LAHN-den]
Vogelpark Walsrode	[FO-gel-pahrk vahls-ROH-deh]
Von Scharnhorst	[fon SHAHRN-horst]
Waldfee	[VAHLD-fay]
Waldtraut Nielsen	[VAHLD-traowt NEEL-sen]
Walküre	[vahl-K(E)OO-reh]
Waltz ®	[vahlts]
Wartburg	[vahrt-boorg]
Wehrinsel	[VEHR-ehn-zel]
Weihenstephan	[VIY-hen-steh-fahn]
Weisse aus Sparrieshoop	[VIY-seh aows SHPAH-rees-hop]
Weisse Grüss an Aachen	[VIY-seh gr(e)oos ahn AH-hkhen]
Weisse Immensee	[VIY-seh EHM-en-zay]
Weisse Margot Koster	[VIY-seh MAHR-got KOS-ter]
Weisse Max Graf ®	[VIY-seh mahx grahf]
Weisse Nelkenrose	[VIY-seh NEHL-ken-ro-zeh]
Weisse New Dawn	[VIY-seh]
Weisse Woge	[VIY-seh voh-geh]
Weisse Wolke ®	[VIY-seh vol-keh]
Weisser Engel	[VIY-ser EHN-gel]

Weisserote Mme Sancy de Parabére	
	[viy-seh-roh-teh]
Wenzel Geschwind	[VEN-tsel-geh-SHVEHND]
Werner Dirks	[VEHR-ner dehrks]
Werner von Blon ®	[VEHR-ner fon blon]
Westerland	[VEHS-ter-lahnd]
Westfalenpark ®	[vehst-FAH-len-pahrk]
White Cécile Brunner	[BROON-ner]

White Gene Boerner	[BUHR-ner]
White Max Graf	[mahx grahf]
White Tausendschön	[TAOW-zend-shuhn]
Wichmoss	[veh(k)h-mos]
Wickwar	[veek-vahr]
Wiedenbrück	[VEE-den-br(e)ook]
Wiener Charme	[VEE-ner shahrm]
Wienerwald ®	[VEE-ner-vahld]
Wildenfelds Gelb	[VEHL-den-fehlds gehlb]
Wildenfelds Rosa	[VEHL-den-fehlds ROH-zah]
Wildenfels gelb	[VEEL-den-fehls gehlb]
Wildfeuer	[VEHLD-foy-er]
Wilhelm	[vehl-hehlm]
Wilhelm Hansmann	[VEHL-hehlm HAHNS-mahn]
Wilhelm	[VEHL-hehlm]
Wilhelmshöhle	[VEHL-hehlms-huh-leh]
Will Alderman	[vehl AHL-der-mahn]
Wörlitz	[vuhr-lehts]
Wurzburg	[voorts-boorg]
Yellow Champagner	[shahm-PAH-n(e)er] ?
Yellow Mozart	[MOH-tsahrt]
Yellow Tausendschön	[taow-zend-shuhn]
Zell	[tsell]
Zieber House of Light Yellow	[TSEE-ber]
Zigeunerblut	[tsee-GOY-ner-bloot]
Zigeunerknabe	[tsee-GOY-ner-KNAH-beh]
Zinger Min	[tsin-ger Min]
Zitronenfalter®	[tsee-troh-nen-fahl-ter]
Zitronenjette ®	[tsee-troh-nen-yeh-teh]
Zukunft	[TSOO-koonft]
Zweibrücken	[tsviy-BR(E)OO-ken]
Zweibrücken	[tsviy-BR(E)OO-ken]
Zwerg	[tsvehrg]
Zwergenfee ®	[TSVEHR-gen-fay]
Zwergkönig	[tsvehrg-KUH-nehg]
Zwergkönigin 82 ®	[tsvehrg-KUH-neh-gehn]

Rose Notes:

Rose Notes:

Rose Notes:

About the Author

Diana Bellucci has always had a passion for her favorite flower, the rose. She remembers her childhood home graced with a few Hybrid Tea roses that her mother planted, including the lovely "Peace" rose. As she designed and planted many rose gardens over time herself, she became fascinated with the history and charm of the antique heirloom roses that led to the Hybrid Tea of today.

As a collector of fine heirloom roses, Diana realized that, because many varieties were cultivated in countries such as France and Germany, they were often named in honor of dignitaries, places or events of their time. This meant that this English-speaking collector was "tongue tied" when trying to order, show, or discuss the 140 different varieties of roses in her garden.

Determined to solve this problem, Diana brought together a team of professional French and German teachers, native Parisians, and Americans to show her how to say the seemingly unpronounceable antique rose names. She compiled what she learned into this reference guide so rose collectors, dealers and hybridizers could also learn how to pronounce the names. Through it, she hopes to give these beautiful antique roses the honor and grace they deserve, and encourage their preservation and proliferation worldwide.

Luminosa Publishing, Inc.

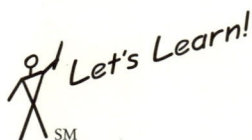

Let's Learn!

SM